Dogs and Children

DOGS AND CHILDREN

Barbara Sykes

THE CROWOOD PRESS

First published in 2002 by
The Crowood Press Ltd
Ramsbury, Marlborough
Wiltshire SN8 2HR

© Barbara Sykes 2002

All rights reserved. No part of this publication may be reproduced or transmitted in any form or by any means, electronic or mechanical, including photocopy, recording, or any information storage and retrieval system, without permission in writing from the publishers.

British Library Cataloguing-in-Publication Data
A catalogue record for this book is available from the British Library.

ISBN 1 86126 489 5

Swindon Borough Council Library Services	
Askews	
636.70887	£9.99

Acknowledgements
I would like to thank Malcolm and Maureen Merone for their patience and photographic skills, Kara and her children Jamie and Hannah for allowing us to take unusual photographs, Chloe for sacrificing her ice cream and Samantha for helping us to photograph early learning scenes with her daughter Hannah. I would also like to thank everyone who has participated in helping us to depict 'special' scenes throughout the book.

Photographs of Sinead and Duster by B. Duggan; Hannah Jo and Ellie by Juliet Walling; and Henry and Hector by Jeremy Wilson. All other photographs by Malcolm and Maureen Merone.

Typeset by Phoenix Typesetting, Ilkley, West Yorkshire

Printed and bound in Great Britain by The Cromwell Press, Trowbridge, Wiltshire

CONTENTS

Introduction		7
1	Facing the Facts	8
2	Making Decisions	15
3	Preparing the Way	22
4	Avoiding Jealousy	32
5	Safe Havens	40
6	First Steps, First Words	52
7	Gaining Respect	65
8	Living, Loving and Learning Together	77
Index		93

INTRODUCTION

Some say children and dogs don't mix, some say they do. You will always hear conflicting information but it is up to the individual to finally decide if they are capable, and want to put in the time needed, to understand and educate dog and child to live together in harmony. Children should not be kept away from nature and if educated to respect animals it can only enhance their growing years, however, if you have the tiniest shadow of doubt about introducing a dog into your family then don't do it.

There is no intention in this book to depict any particular breed of dog as being recommended or otherwise as a family dog. However, some photographs have been orchestrated to depict a particular scene so dogs we know, or have trained ourselves, have been photographed with children who are used to dogs. The photographs are a visual aid to explain certain circumstances and scenarios. By working with children and dogs known to us we have been able to provide explicit photographs showing events that could lead to an undesirable conclusion. The exception is Hannah Matthews, seen on the cover with Skye and inside the book with Skye and Rob. She has not been photographed with any dog in order to provide cute photographs, Hannah is still young and Rob is trained not to push or jump near children. Skye who is on the front cover is gentle and doesn't play with a ball. Instead she looks to children for gentle instruction and not games. If you study the cover photograph carefully you will see that Hannah is not standing in front of Skye, but sideways, which offers no threat to the dog and helps in preventing any close eye contact. Her body is relaxed and she knows that she is not to hug or cuddle but instead to become friends with Skye; however, a simple piece of grass in her left hand that she has been asked not to let go of, helps her to resist any temptation to do so.

This book is not about training dogs. It is about children with dogs and I am not advocating that everyone should rush out and buy a dog for their child. On the contrary, there are far too many cases of children being bitten and of dogs being put down because they are 'not safe' with children. These problems do not 'happen', they are 'created', and the following chapters explain *how they are created*, and *how to avoid them*.

Any breed or size of dog can be a problem or a pal but they are not toys, and children must be taught to revere them and to be proud of them. If a child is wanting a dog to play with, it is the wrong reason for having a dog. But if a child is educated to love and respect a dog, and a dog is taught its correct place in your pack, then the wonder of nature and magic of a special kind of friend are waiting to be born.

CHAPTER 1

FACING THE FACTS

There is an old saying 'never work with animals and children', but animals and children have a marvellous acceptance of life. They don't try to see beyond the obvious, they don't plot their future and they have a natural respect of the unknown. Adults know there must be some form of order, some continuity and some discipline, so they begin to explain this to the children and the animals, but if they order rather than explain they leave themselves wide open to argument. In the case of children the argument can be two-sided as there is a common language, but in the case of animals the argument often results in insubordination, the animal appearing to be disobedient. This will cause the adult human to feel frustrated and the animal will probably be bombarded with more orders, thus causing an even larger gap in the communication barrier. Both the animal, in this instance a dog, and the child need guidance, they need a set of rules to live by. In the wild the animal will receive this from its parents and its pack leader, just as a child will learn from its parents. But humans are more complicated than dogs, they have the rules of the country they live in, the rules of their immediate area, rules passed down through generations and rules that others bestow on them. Everywhere we look we are confronted with rules, in books, on the back of doors, in offices, in schools, on public transport, the list is endless and quite often can confuse our own set of personal rules, the ones we need to teach our children. We know what we want to teach and how we want our children to behave but we also have to prepare them for the rules of school, that may be different from the rules of home. Without realizing it we can end up being the person who gives orders but does not listen.

A child and a dog can learn from each other and they can benefit from living and growing together. They need rules and they need supervision but the beauty of a relationship between a child and a dog is that they listen to each other, they have time for each other and they are always there for each other. In the adult world of instability, rules and regulations, a child and a dog can enter their own private world where time stands still, magic is all around and there begins to materialize a wonderful relationship of trust, respect and friendship. It is the relationship that any parent who brings a child and a dog together dreams of but unfortunately it can so often end in disappointment. This can often be attributed to the adult's failure to decide how the relationship should be rather than guiding and nurturing it and then allowing it to take its course.

Life is about balance, the harder we work the more we need to relax. If we use our brain at work during the day then an evening working in the garden or DIY

FACING THE FACTS

Under supervision the innocence of a puppy and a child combined can give moments to be remembered, but it does not just 'happen', it has to be worked at.

can provide the balance needed. Dogs need to be trained, they need a set of rules and they must respect their pack leader, but their training or education must be balanced. If they spend time learning a strenuous activity they will balance themselves with rest, this is their natural way of keeping fit and alert. In the wild their very existence depends on their ability to think, work within the pack but still be able to use their initiative. If left to work things out for themselves they both can and will organize their own life around ours, fit in with our way of life and abide by our rules but still be individuals.

Children are given rules to live by within the family unit and once these rules are understood there become grey areas in which they can live. These are areas where a child can work things out for itself, perhaps bending the rules a little but not breaking them. For example, there may be a rule that says it is impolite to take the last biscuit especially when there are visitors to the home. However, taking the last biscuit from a plate when no visitors are present and there are more biscuits in the tin is not really bad-mannered or breaking a rule. The child learns by progression. To begin with, the biscuit will be ignored but as the child matures it will ask if it can take the last biscuit. When it is mature and sensible enough to live in the grey area it will know when and when not to take a biscuit. Children are encouraged to work situations out for themselves and to be creative. This good parenting can be extended to dog training for dogs are also capable of working things out for themselves, but unfortunately we often tend to restrict their thought process by issuing orders without giving them a chance to think.

Dogs do need to be obedient and there are certain commands they must not question but if we are going to provide the balance necessary for a happy well-adjusted dog then we must also provide the dog with the opportunity to use its brain and to be creative. The dog that works hard and then rests when it is tired is exercising its right to be an individual

FACING THE FACTS

Dogs are like children when they are playing, they can become over excited and behave out of character. A big dog like this one could harm a child just by knocking him or her over, and if it were to run toward a child who is a stranger behaving in such a manner, it could trigger off a series of events instigated by fear that could have serious repercussions.

within the pack. But if we play with a dog and keep it playing beyond the point of tiredness then, like a child, it will become over excited. Just as a child will end up in tears when over tired the dog will inevitably upset its owners, and when *they* are tired of playing it will not be able to understand or wind down. It has been dictated to, it was told when to play, how long for and when to stop; if this were for important training then it would be work, but when playing the dog should be able to make some decisions. No doubt it appears to *want* to play but does it know how to stop playing? I have had people approach me regarding their dog because it either won't play or only plays for a short time, they see this as a problem but what is really happening is that the dog is not performing as and when they want.

If a dog and a child are brought up with sensible rules and allowed to work things out they will each know when to leave the other alone. A dog that is allowed to play with a ball and becomes over excited or even reaches exhaustion point is going to be a liability if a child comes on the scene. A child who is allowed all its own way and is used to demanding games as and when it wants, is a child that should be kept well out of the way of dogs thus avoiding a situation that could end up in heartbreak. A dog is a dog and a child is a child, neither can be trusted with the other 100 per cent. A child who lacks respect for parents or discipline is likely to instigate an accident even with the most mild-mannered dog, and a dog that has not been taught to accept children as hierarchy will see no harm in treating them with disrespect.

Opinions vary greatly on the subject of children and dogs in the same house. I have heard many state quite confidently that, 'children and dogs just don't mix', and I also know of many children who have benefited greatly from having a dog as their 'best friend'. Those who believe they should be kept apart have often an underlying reason other than an educated opinion. They may have had a bad experience previously with a dog, they may not feel confident or have the time to train

FACING THE FACTS

a dog, or in some cases they are not really dog lovers. Unfortunately, these opinions are often taken on board by people seeking advice born of experience and not prejudice, thus casting doubt over their own capabilities of successfully combining child and dog and creating a wonderful learning curve for both.

It is right to question, seek advice and consider very seriously whether or not to bring a dog into a family where children are, or are anticipated to be. If doubt persists, then it is better to err on the side of caution and wait until more information emerges or more confidence built up. However the final decision whether to take a dog into the family is up to the family concerned. It is important when reading books and listening to advice that all the information received does not become so mixed up and contradictory that common sense fails to prevail. It's rather like building a wall and asking people to supply you with some bricks – you will receive more than you need and some won't even be the right ones for the type of wall you are building. You discard immediately all the unsuitable ones, hang on to the maybes and begin to build with the definites. If, as you build, you keep throwing bricks in at random, your wall will be weak. You only use the maybes if they appear to be needed and stick to building the wall with an eye for what is sensible and going to provide the desired end result. The parenting of children and the training of a dog if nothing else have one thing in common – they both need a good dose of common sense!

Throughout this book we will inject common-sense training into many different scenarios, for although children and dogs can gain so much from each other they can also do each other great harm if

Unlike a big dog this chap will not be jumping up at anybody's face but he is still capable of becoming over excited or over tired. Dogs are not toys or teddy bears and if a child has not been taught to consider a dog's feelings then discomfort can be caused.

not understood and educated to live together in harmony. Situations can vary greatly and problems can arise whether dealing with a puppy or an older dog, a toddler or a teenager. If you are already blessed with dogs and children the question of when and where to begin does not arise. Many couples already have a dog when they start a family and whereas for some there are few problems, others find jealousy and possessiveness rearing their

FACING THE FACTS

heads when their dog suddenly finds it is no longer the centre of attention. Families without dogs often ponder on the ideal time to introduce a dog into the household – believe me there is no ideal time. If you are going to wait for the right moment you will be waiting forever – it's rather like waiting to start a family, isn't it? Time, money, circumstance all provide pros and cons until suddenly you realize you are listening to all points of view rather than heeding your own feelings and wishes. When you cut out any outside influence and listen to your inner self you will know when you are ready to take a dog into your home and your life. If one little part of you thinks it is not right then don't do it. This dog is for life not just for the time it takes to find out it was a bad idea and the timing was wrong. You need to take everything into consideration – lifestyle, holidays, general interests of the family and then think carefully about what is entailed in introducing a dog into this environment. It is not a machine, toy or object that can be put aside when there are more important things to attend to; it is a living being and as such must be allocated a place amongst those important things.

If you already share your life with a dog and your family is about to increase in number the dog needs to be prepared for the big occasion. Resentment can be avoided by providing it with a place of its own where it can amuse itself contentedly whilst visitors dote on the new arrival. When a new baby arrives everyone and everything around changes – routine, feelings and emotions take a complete about turn, but don't expect a dog to understand this. All a dog understands is that the time and energy once spent on him is now redirected. It is up to the ones who know the reason for the change, the humans, to make sure that although the routine may be different the dog is still a part of their lives.

The important thing is to make sure that all aspects of bringing a dog into the family have been considered and that any uncertainties are dealt with before and not after making a final decision. I strongly advise anyone who has or is about to have a new baby to put aside any thoughts of adding a dog to the family for quite some time. No matter how well equipped you may be as dog owners or how capable of training a dog, a baby takes a lot of looking after, as does a dog. In much the same way I will advise anyone with a puppy to wait until it is a little older before getting another puppy. Time and patience have to be divided between the two and the strong, loyal and affectionate bond created between dog and owner often fails to materialize as the division of time and loyalties means neither dog is getting 100 per cent concentration and dedication in their upbringing. During the day, the baby needs constant attention and the sleeping periods will not last. Before long the whole day will be spent with a child who hardly rests. It is not enough to take the dog out for a walk and give it attention at the end of the day when both partners are at home, for strange as it may seem, this can often make the dog more restless. It has to sit and take a back seat all day to a baby, but it is able to see and hear its owners and it can see and hear the baby – it is excluded from the activity but not from the scene. A puppy needs to have time spent with it but it must be quality time. Your presence there all day is not enough – it needs to learn and to understand. In other words, it needs education.

If there is already a dog on the scene when the baby arrives then it will probably be older and that bonding of understanding will have already been created between dog and owners. Bringing an older dog into the family where there is a new baby, in the hope that it will enable it to enter the family without quite so much time dedicated to it, can be unfair on the dog. An older dog must be given almost the same consideration as a puppy; it may be older but it is 'new born' into your family, your home, your environment and your rules.

Introducing a dog when the child is a toddler can also have its setbacks. How well-educated is the child already regarding animals? How well-behaved is the child? Does the child respect toys, teddy bears and house rules? If a child has no respect for toys, handling them roughly and breaking them, then there is a strong possibility that a dog may suffer similar harsh treatment, particularly if the dog is the first animal the child has had real contact with and no previous pet education has been forthcoming. Another consideration is the possibility of more children. If the toddler is the youngest child then the house may be full of visiting children of mixed ages. If the toddler is the first child then any additional children will mean coping with toddler, baby and dog!

It may seem easy to work out a routine that suits everyone – after all at the end of a working day both parents will be at home and one will be free to walk the dog whilst the other looks after the children. Even if the novelty of having a dog to walk never wears off, it is not fair to expect a dog to take a back seat all day with no time or education being given to it simply because you want a dog. Granted, not all breeds of dog demand the same amount of attention but young, old, fat, thin, fast or slow they all deserve both time and respect. This is not to say it is impossible. I reared kids, dogs, calves and goodness knows what as well as allocating time for my partner but believe me it was not easy. I know many families who have successfully brought up kids and dogs together but not without a great deal of thought and in many cases sacrifice. That blissful hour of peace and quiet when a fractious baby or toddler finally settles will not be yours for the taking when you have a dog patiently waiting and just as deserving of your time.

It doesn't matter if a person has shared their life previously with many dogs of different breeds, it doesn't matter if they are an accomplished dog trainer and neither does it matter if they are familiar with raising children. Dogs and children in the same home and sharing the same family, car, garden and life cannot be expected to behave in the same way as they would living apart. It takes a lot of soul-searching to make the right decision and if that decision is to unite the two in one family then it takes a lot of hard work to get it right. Any family introducing a dog into their lives needs to make sure they understand all the implications, for a mistake with a dog can sometimes be rectified by extra training but it may be left too late and the dog has to be rehomed. It is imperative that mistakes are foreseen and overcome when a child is involved for that mistake can cost dearly. Unfortunately there are far too many accidents involving children and dogs each year, but if only one accident a year resulted from an insufficient knowledge of understanding dogs with children then it is one too many. It is one dog destroyed and one child scarred for life, mentally and physically.

There are many advantages to children growing up with animals in that they can be made aware of their needs and learn

FACING THE FACTS

how to care for them. A little extra soul-searching, a large portion of serious training for both dog and child, a dash of honesty when needed, mixed with common sense and topped with a lot of understanding and the recipe for that magic child and dog relationship is almost ready. So let's start to prepare it and make sure it is applied with a liberal dose of fun as well.

Chapter Summary

It doesn't matter how much a dog may be wanted, it is important to consider a dog's needs, for both time and patience are as important for the dog as for children.

Being a good dog owner in the past and being good with children does not necessarily mean that a person is well equipped to deal with them both together on a permanent basis.

Dogs and children have much to give and to learn from each other but if they are not brought up to respect each other, problems will arise.

No dog should enter a family on a trial basis so if any member of the family has doubts, then it is safer, kinder and wiser to wait until such time as the dog can enter the family on a happy and permanent basis.

CHAPTER 2

MAKING DECISIONS

When faced with the decision of whether or not the time is right to introduce a dog into your family life, a great deal of thought must also be given to the type of dog that will be right for you and the kind of life you can promise it.

The purchase of a new car can be an agonizing decision. Colour and make may play an important part but the fuel consumption, reliability and type such as saloon, hatchback, estate or van are all important criteria. The same forethought must be applied when choosing a dog; it is not sufficient to pick a dog from a rescue centre or a puppy from a litter on appearance alone, they must be right for you and capable of fitting into your lifestyle. I cannot stress enough the importance of selecting the dog that is right for you, and not necessarily the dog you *believe* to be right for you.

You may have always wanted a very large breed of dog but if you live in a small house this may be not be practicable. If you have children a large dog will not be easy to contain in a small area in the garden or the house. However, opting for a smaller breed will not necessarily resolve any problems that may arise with a larger dog. Some small breeds can be quite quick-tempered and just as a large dog may suffer from a lack of privacy a small dog can suffer at the hands of children who see it more as a toy than a living being.

You will have children and dog under your roof for a long time so make every effort to ensure that if you go ahead with the decision to include a dog in your family it is going to be the dog for everyone and not a dog that just suits an individual whim. This dog is not knocking on your door and asking to join you, it is not given a choice, so be absolutely certain that you are committed to the dog, its welfare, its training, its needs and the needs of the rest of the family.

Quite often a dog is already established in a family before children arrive, in which case the selection of breed or character is not optional. The dog may have belonged to one of the partners before they became a family unit in which case it has to make two major adjustments in its life. One, when it has to share its owner with their partner and then later, perhaps, it must learn to share them both with a baby. This dog may have the advantage of being established and, hopefully, of being trained, but it also has major adjustments to make. The dog entering the family after the arrival of children will be entering a new life and will not have any comparisons or jealousies to deal with but it will need training and, like a child, constant reminding of the rules.

Hard Facts

We already have some hard facts to face. It is not right to have a particular breed of dog just because it is the breed one

MAKING DECISIONS

When choosing a breed of dog it is important to take into account the kind of lifestyle and accommodation you can offer, for example, a large breed will need spacious accommodation. However large or small the body, the mind is still that of a dog and needs educating as such. There are a variety of breeds and sizes in this picture but they are all well-behaved dogs, you must make sure that you are able to provide the time needed to educate your dog.

member of the family would prefer. Neither is it right or fair to expect a dog to sit and wait all day for one partner to come home and exercise it because the other has not the time. If there is not the time for a dog then it should not be in the family! Having owned a dog previously does not necessarily mean that any difficulties will be recognized and overcome, for a dog in a family environment is different from a dog in a one-on-one environment.

It is true that if someone has already had the experience of sharing their life with a dog then they will have some knowledge to draw on. But how long ago was it and in what circumstances? Growing up with a dog may have been a wonderful experience but it would probably have been your parents who trained the dog and it may have been a long time ago. You may be confident but your partner may not; they may even have suffered a frightening experience from a dog in the past. However experienced and knowledgeable about responsible dog ownership a person may be it is a whole new ball game when children are involved. There is nothing easy in bringing up children; it is a huge learning curve and one where mistakes are inevitable. Children cry, fall ill, have tantrums and require endless patience. They will often react adversely when the

MAKING DECISIONS

A 'child-free' corner of your garden is a wonderful safe haven for your dog where he can do all the things dogs love to do. You can even provide him with his own digging area just as Dave is doing here with Sapho. This will leave the main part of your garden as a clean and hygienic area for children to play in.

babysitter arrives and you are late for your important meeting with the result that your patience is being tested to its limits. Can you cope with all this and more, still having endless time and patience left for a dog? If you do not have the time to read a book, go for a walk, take a leisurely drive, if you do not have any quality time for yourself or your partner, if the thought of having another child would mean that you just couldn't cope, then you are not ready for, or in a position to bring a dog into your family. Not a large, small, or even very tiny one, since all dogs need and deserve the same amount of time. Being small does not mean deserving of less time, it simply means smaller in body but still with the mind of a dog.

A Time for Honesty

We often know how we would like a situation to be and if we are lucky we may be able to create that ideal, but if the correct facilities are not available then no amount of wishing or working can make it happen. So it is the responsibility of every potential dog owner to be honest about the facilities they can provide for a dog. A dog needs its own space so if your house is only tiny or you live in a flat, where can you create a child-free zone for your dog? Most homes, large or small, can be rearranged to create a dog-free zone for the baby but small houses will rarely stand two areas being cordoned off. A garden really is a must, a dog needs to have some personal freedom, somewhere it can be peaceful, chew a bone, doze or dig, and it also needs a retreat. You cannot just think short-term either, for as the baby grows into a toddler and then a small child, your house will be an entertainment base for parties, and playtimes to many children, not just your own. Your dog may enjoy this company, but there is no guarantee it will, and it should not be subjected to the small invasive hands of other children who may not understand or be used to dogs. A yard is not a good substitute for a garden, dogs like grass and they like to lie on something cool in summer. A hard surface is often advisable in a dog run so that in wet weather the dog is not subjected to mud and puddles but a grassy area for warm summer days is natural to a dog and will make it happy.

How important do you deem good manners in children? Do you intend to endeavour to teach your own children, good manners? If you already have children, are they good mannered? What would be your reaction if you visited a friend's home and your children began to wander around the room, interrupted the conversation and picked up ornaments from the shelf? If none of the aforementioned seem important or if your children lapse regularly into bad manners in other people's homes then you are going to have difficulty in understanding and portraying the leadership qualities needed to educate and train a young dog. This is not meant to offend, no two families are alike and manners and rules are for the individuals to set but when it comes to dogs there is only one set of rules and that is the one that dogs understand, pack rules. The time for honesty is not when a mistake is realized and a dog is up for adoption because it does not fit into the family lifestyle or the owners did not understand its requirements. The time for honesty is *before* making the decision to have a dog and all members of the family concerned must be honest with each other. Far too many dogs have been chosen because a child was adamant that they would look after it and take it for walks, but children change and they do not always realize just what they are promising. It may make parents unpopular for a time but it is better to face up to the fact that the child may change its mind, to say no and be unpopular for a while than to deal with the heart-ache of an unwanted or undisciplined dog.

Why Do You Want a Dog?

We have already covered the need for all members of the family to be in agreement and for all to want a dog. If just one member of the family does not want the dog then it is inadvisable to go ahead with the decision to bring one into the family. If an adult member of the family is against having a dog it will always be a 'bone of contention' when the going gets tough. It may not like the babysitter, it may annoy the baby, pinch its toys, take up too much time or simply vie for affection, but it will be the dog that suffers and it will be the dog that has to go if life becomes unbearable. Sadly, I have known many families who have been through the above scenario and after the dog has been rehomed they have realized how much they missed it, how much they instigated its problems and of course are left with feelings of guilt. These are not thoughtless people, neither are they cruel or unkind, they simply don't realize how much time and effort are required to look after a dog and how much a dog can be affected by its environment. Dogs will react to what they see and what they are taught; a dog in a house of dispute is a dog in dispute!

If a child is either against bringing a dog into the family or doesn't understand the implications and the seriousness of owning a dog, and believe me a child is never too young to learn, then the dog could be subjected to adverse treatment at a later date. A child who shares responsibility for the welfare of the dog will look after it and will protect it from unwelcome advances from other less animal-educated

MAKING DECISIONS

Most children love being given responsibility. Being encouraged to participate in the training of the family dog is not only a wonderful experience but also a learning curve for them. If a child is not willing to be a responsible dog owner then the time is not right to introduce a dog into your family.

children. But a child who does not want this responsibility, or who is not prepared to take it seriously, will fail to notice any distress the dog may be suffering at the hands of visiting friends. As I mentioned before, no dog knocks on our door asking to live with us. It is the responsibility of each individual to be absolutely honest before the dog enters the home; it is too late afterwards, for no matter how guilty or sorry a human being feels it is too late for the dog. It will already be an unwanted pet.

Before any decision can be made about taking a dog into the family you have to ask yourselves why you actually want a dog. Perhaps the husband is feeling left out when the children arrive, or believes that he will have time on his hands whilst his wife is occupied with the children. A wife and mother may feel that she needs something to give her a reason for going out in the evening and taking some exercise. Children often want a dog without understanding any of the implications of care or parents think a dog will keep the children occupied playing together whilst they are busy. None of these come anywhere close to being even half a valid reason for getting a dog! You have to really *feel* that you want a dog; it comes from deep inside and it doesn't go, so if the time is not right now, there *will* be a right time later. I remember overhearing a conversation in a supermarket some time ago. Two children asked their father if they could buy a toy. He told them that the toys were not for children but for dogs. The children then asked if they could have a dog and their father replied, 'I don't see why not. We'll ask your mum when we get home and if she says yes we'll come back and get some toys for it.' This held no *feeling* about getting an animal. This was supermarket shopping and even if the gentleman had no intention of getting a dog he was not showing a responsible attitude to the children. But then when dog 'accessories' are displayed in supermarkets it is inevitable that children will begin asking questions.

MAKING DECISIONS

The couple who already have a dog when a baby arrives have just as much soul-searching and honesty to face. For long before the baby arrives, in fact before it is even conceived, the preparation of the dog for the ensuing change in its life cannot begin soon enough. The dog will have been the centre of attention most of the time; it will have been taken for walks, played with, spoken to, taken on car drives and in general will have been an integrated family member, it may even have achieved hierarchy status in its own eyes. Suddenly all this changes, the conversation is aimed at or around a small and very noisy bundle and the walks become infrequent. This may only be for a few days during a settling in period of adjustment but you can't explain that to the dog! It is far kinder and ultimately safer for the dog to be introduced to a new routine when you have the time to help it to adjust. If the dog is not well-mannered and has gained a hierarchy position within your unit then you must work very hard to rectify the situation before the baby arrives. Both your time and patience will be short afterwards and the dog will have more than enough time to begin harbouring resentment.

Have I painted a picture of doom and gloom? Probably, and it may have put you off having a dog or if you already have one you may be scurrying off to the local

If a dog has been used to getting all the attention it will try every trick it can think of to divert your attention from your child. Copper is trying to take Pat's attention away from Chloe but he is about to be told to sit down and wait his turn.

MAKING DECISIONS

bookshop to find a book on dog training. I am not deliberately trying to dissuade anyone from bringing up dogs and children together but if someone can be dissuaded then perhaps they are not really committed to dog ownership or know they are not yet ready to take on the extra responsibility. It is responsible to admit that the time is not right and it is irresponsible to go ahead and get a dog knowing full well that you have reservations about either the timing or indeed about having a dog at all.

When a child and dog live in the same house and either one is disrespectful towards the other I have no qualms about saying that the situation can be an accident waiting to happen. At no time should a dog be allowed to believe it is either hierarchy or littermate to a child and at no time should a child be allowed to treat a dog as if it were a toy. At no time should a small child and a dog be left together unsupervised and at no time should a dog be left to play with a group of visiting children.

When a child and a dog share a life together and a bond is created they will be constant companions but this does not just happen, it needs the right dog, the right atmosphere, the right education and even then it is important to remember that a child is young and can be irresponsible and that a dog is a dog. No matter how good the child is or how well-behaved and well-trained the dog, never trust either of them 100 per cent! Adults make mistakes, they lose patience and sometimes their tempers, a child can throw a totally unexpected tantrum and even lash out. These lapses, even in normally placid adults and children, happen but they pass and explanations and apologies can help to repair any bad feeling. When a dog has a lapse an apology is not an option, for a child can be maimed for life and the dog may be put down as a result.

To help prevent any such recipes for disaster it's time to look at how forethought, time and patience can make the dream of that special bond a reality.

Chapter Summary

When thinking of taking a dog into your family all members of the family must be in agreement. Having owned a dog previously does not necessarily mean that it will be easy a second time; running a family is time consuming and a large portion of both time and patience will need to be allotted to the dog.

Good manners must be high on the list of priorities for children and the dog. It is important to be honest about your reasons for wanting a dog for it will not be knocking on your door and asking for accommodation. It will not be given a choice so you must be absolutely sure that you will not let it down.

If you already have a dog, do not wait until your first baby is born to introduce the dog to a new regime; it will not understand and may harbour resentment.

CHAPTER 3

PREPARING THE WAY

Preparing the way for a dog entering a family with children, or for a couple who are about to have a family and need their dog to accept the newcomer, is essential. But it is also important to take into account anyone else who may be involved either with the welfare and training of the dog or with relations and baby-sitters of the children. For example it may not have mattered too much if a relation is allergic to dogs but if a new baby arrives and that relation happens to be a doting grandparent who lives near enough to be making regular visits then they must be taken into consideration. Have you a choice of several baby-sitters or just one? If just the one make sure they are not afraid of, or allergic to dogs. It is your home, your family and it will be your dog but when children are involved there will be other considerations to take into account.

It is also important to prepare yourselves for the event, whether it is a new dog being introduced into the family or a dog being introduced to a new baby. It is up to the adults of the family to set an example to the children, and if they are seen to be unsure or they make too much fuss of the dog the children will be either nervous or over excited. The dog needs to settle and to get used to its surroundings, do you have a place for it to go? and, are you prepared to defend its privacy against the intrusion of your children?

If you are about to have a baby are you prepared for the change in feelings? Before the baby is born you may be absolutely certain you will still feel the same toward your dog and that there will be no problem allotting time each day for him. But what seemed important on Monday can suddenly pale into insignificance on Tuesday simply because a baby came home and you were not prepared for the change in your priorities. If you take these things into consideration and deal with them before the event, preparing yourself mentally for any changes, then it will help to make things run smoothly during the first few days.

Preparing to Bring a New Dog into the Family

When you feel you have thought through all the pros and cons and are certain that the time is right for you to get a dog there are yet more decisions to be made. Where is this dog going to come from? and, will it be a puppy or an older dog? How old are the children in your family? and, how capable are they of taking on board all that is necessary to provide a safe and educational environment for a dog?

Whatever breed of dog you decide on remember that it has to be manageable by all members of the family. Large dogs can pull or knock over small or young children

PREPARING THE WAY

No matter how small and cute a puppy may be it will soon grow into a full-size adult dog. Make sure when you choose a puppy that you know how big it will be when it is fully grown.

and they need a large area of their own in the home and garden. All dogs need regular exercise but a small dog can obtain a reasonable amount of exercise in a garden whereas a large dog will be limited for exercise even in a large garden. Small dogs take up less space and they are more manageable for children in regard to size and strength but they may not fit in with the energetic kind of life some families may lead.

If you are looking for a puppy remember that no matter how small and cute it appears when it is with its mother it will grow into a full size adult dog very soon. If its parents are large dogs then the puppy will be similar in size to them at maturity, however, this may be the only guarantee you can have of it following in their pawprints. In theory if the parents are gentle-natured one would think the offspring should be similar, but like humans, puppies can take after other ancestors. So it is important that you check other family members; if you cannot check the grandparents or puppies from previous litters and have no independent verbal references then you would be well advised to select from another source. The good breeding of the puppy takes you on your way to having a good dog but believe me the onus is not on the breeder alone. Bad handling can spoil good dogs and dogs of dubious nature can become reliable companions, however when children come into the equation there is no room for a dog of known unreliable nature in your home. When I talk of good breeding I am not referring to champion dogs, it is the soundness and reliability of the breedline that is important, not the number of accolades the parents and grandparents have notched up. What is more important – a dog that has champion parents but may have an uncertain temperament, or a dog from good parents that have a reputation for being solid and reliable? Dogs as well as humans need to be honest, and a dishonest or sneaky dog can win a competition making it worth a substantial amount of money, but an honest dog is worth its weight in gold. It goes without saying many prize winners are honest and reliable but don't let the accolades blind you to the real dog.

If you think you would prefer not to go through puppy training and are considering an older dog, you may find that you need to spend as much if not more time with it than with a puppy. Older dogs are usually rescues or unwanted dogs and many of them have problems due to the lack of stability in their lives. Having said this there are many rescue dogs in need of a good home and provided they are not aggressive they can be re-educated to become well-mannered responsive dogs. Unfortunately quite often dogs are placed into rescue because they have proved to be unreliable with children; this may be no fault of the dog's, other than being in the wrong home at the wrong time. But if children have annoyed or harassed it or if it has proved too time-consuming for the family to train it correctly then problems will have developed. If you are taking in a rescue do make sure you get all the correct background information before making a decision. For if a dog has not settled with a family and you are not in a position to give it the necessary training, it will only suffer if it has to be taken back into rescue. Also, unless your children are old enough to understand that the dog will need more specialized care and attention and that there may be problems ahead that will require them to be patient, then a problem dog is not really an option. If your children are small then you really must concentrate on a dog that has a good and known temperament, but remember there are no guarantees and there is no such thing as 100 per cent reliable. Human beings have days when they do not feel amiable but they can explain this, whereas a dog cannot. A dog is not a robot – it has feelings, it has moods, it can be hurt and it can be over enthusiastic. So try to make sure you are getting a dog with a steady nature and then be prepared to work hard doing the breeder and the dog justice by making sure you teach it good manners.

Choosing a Dog or Puppy

I would strongly recommend that when you first go to look at a dog or a puppy you leave the children behind. This is not a time for letting the heart rule the head and a child will quite often select a dog or puppy for the wrong reasons. It is difficult for an adult to say no to the dog in a rescue kennel looking forlorn and dejected, or the puppy who appears to choose you and won't leave you alone. So the added pleas of a younger generation may serve to sway a sensible decision in favour of one that you know is not really right, for you feel that the tears and pleading cannot be refused. Believe me the path to a well-trained dog will not run smoothly and to allow the heart to rule the head can lead to that poor dejected-looking dog going back into rescue and being even more confused, or the puppy being a delinquent.

If you are choosing a rescue do not be side-tracked into considering a dog you have previously thought to be wrong for your lifestyle. For example, the large dog in a kennel that appears to be quiet and desperately in need of a good home, but when it is fit, healthy and feeling confident in its new home it will be a big strong dog quite capable of pulling or knocking

PREPARING THE WAY

If you are thinking of having a rescue dog, make sure you have done your research and know what kind of a dog is best for you. It is very difficult to be detached when you look at a row of forlorn faces each waiting to be chosen. Dogs need to go to a permanent home and if you choose with your heart and not your head, the dog you so lovingly took into your home may have to go back into rescue if he cannot adapt to your lifestyle.

children over. However, by now you have done all the correct soul-searching and are confident you know what you can and can't cope with and what is right for your circumstances and lifestyle (if you have not, then you are not yet ready to choose a dog), so what changes when you walk through the door of the rescue kennels? Nothing, if a large dog was wrong on the way in then it is wrong on the way out. By all means take time for a discussion but go home to do it and ask yourself have you really thought everything through. I cannot stress enough that the decision will be difficult and the training time-consuming, but you must accept what you as a family are going to be capable of doing and stick to what you believe to be right.

Similarly if your children are old enough to be able to understand and help to train a larger dog, stay away from a very big or strong breed, stick to a medium-sized dog and don't be tempted by the sweet cuddly little toy breed you may see. The novelty of having a small dog will soon wear with the realization that it will not be able to do all the things that had been planned for a dog of more robust stature. I am not going to advise on the size, type or breed of dog

PREPARING THE WAY

to choose if the family includes a baby or baby on the way. I have brought up two children of my own and looked after countless friends of theirs when they have visited, so I understand the problems that can arise, as my dogs were already a part of my life when my children were born. Because we were on a farm and my children were used to the responsibility of having animals I knew that as they grew older they could be relied upon to make sure the dogs were not harassed by visiting friends. Even so it was never easy juggling time schedules, kids, parties and outings at the same time as training and exercising the dogs. So if you have a baby and no dog I would be the last person to advise you to take on the extra responsibility too soon. Being patient for just a while longer can be beneficial for both family and dog and the time lost in waiting can be compensated for by the time available for the whole family, dog included, to spend together.

Parents are the ones paying the food and vet bills, parents are the ones left to exercise the dog when the children go on holiday or stay with friends, so parents are the ones to make the final decision. During any discussions about having a dog, until the parents are certain about what they are going to do then the children need not be brought into the equation other than to sound out their feelings about the possibility of having a dog in the family. If parents are quite sure that they are not ready to have a dog then they must not let their children persuade them otherwise. No doubt there will be cases when this has happened successfully but for every happy outcome made on a rash decision there will be 100 unhappy ones. When parents feel the time is right and have discussed all the problems and possibilities, the children can be included; they can join in discussions, give opinions and help to make decisions. When parents have seen a dog or a puppy that they think is right for them the children can then take part in the final visit, the purchase and the homecoming. Parents can guide their children to 'choose' the dog or puppy that they already feel is right for them. But if they have not already had a chance to view the prospective newcomer quietly and sensibly on their own, then they will find it difficult guiding enthusiastic children and making decisions in one go.

Don't be fooled into thinking a puppy chooses you – it is simply inquisitive, the most forward of the puppy pack and wants to investigate you. This pup may also be a handful! The dog in the rescue kennels who looks at you with soulful eyes *may* be just right for you, but if he is nervous and introvert and your family is noisy and extrovert then you are not doing the dog any favours by choosing him. Your intentions may be good but the outcome could prove traumatic for the dog.

New Baby and the Family Dog

If you are used to dogs and yours is well-mannered there is no reason why any problems should occur. However, if the dog's training is such that it perceives itself to be in control or to have leadership of your pack at any time then problems will most certainly occur. If a dog is unruly or disobedient, then it is obvious that much work will need to be done to remedy this situation before the baby arrives. Quite often a dog may not appear to have problems but when its good manners are really put to the test it may

PREPARING THE WAY

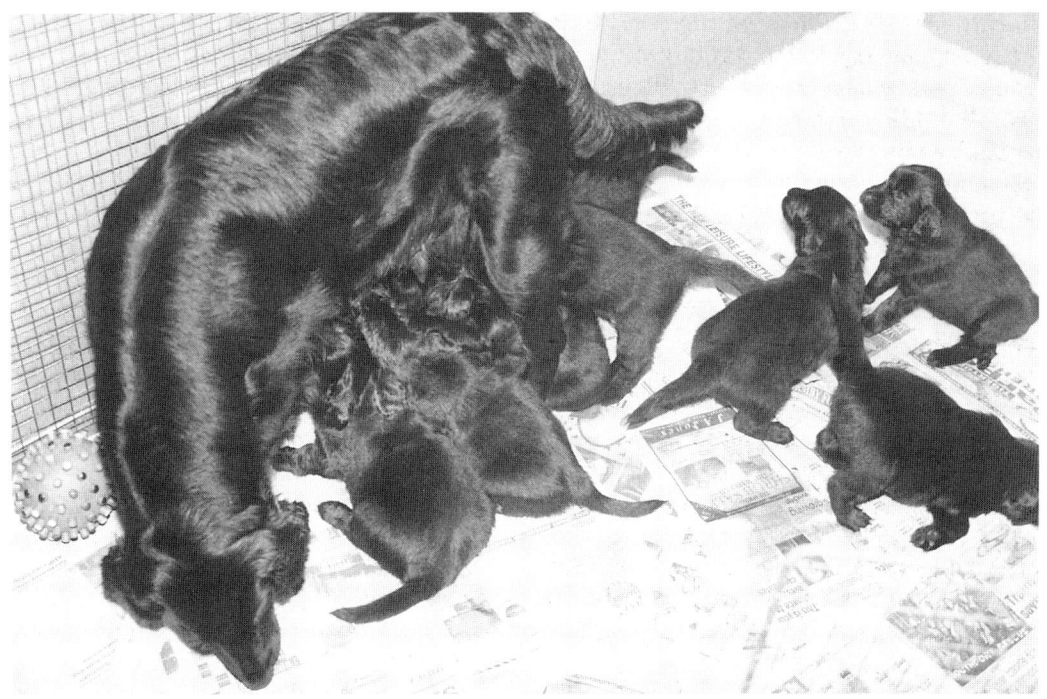

Although your children should be included in the choosing of a new dog it is often wiser to make the first visit without them, especially if it is to see a litter of puppies. Puppies are appealing and children can be persuasive. If you see the litter first you can prepare and guide your children into a sensible decision. The litter in the picture may all look alike but their characters will be different, so you need time to study them to help make the correct choice.

not come through with flying colours. No-one likes to be told that their dog is bad mannered when they are quite sure it is the epitome of perfection. But if it is to be a responsible canine member of a family that is shortly to welcome the addition of a baby, then the prospective parents must be responsible in accepting that just maybe they have let their canine best friend get away with a little too much freedom. It is not so much the fact that the dog may be getting away with a few minor misdemeanours as that it will begin to think it has a right to make you wait on him a little. Does he have an instant recall? Does he walk sensibly on a lead? Does he wait his turn and not push ahead at doors and gates? Does he always look to you for guidance and protection? In short *is* he a real jewel or do you *think* he is. If a dog does not come back when it is called it is making its own decisions. Coming back on the second or third recall is not good enough, if you call him then you should expect him to come, why else would you call him? If he doesn't, then why should he take notice of anything else you say if he doesn't particularly want to? Think how you would feel if each time you asked a child to do something he ignored you. Would you really just keep on repeating your request or would you make it clear that he is displaying bad manners and you are not going to accept it? Remember what I said earlier about good manners – they are important in both child and dog. If you are visiting someone and your dog pulls you into the house, molests the people in there and then investigates every corner of the room, then you have some serious training to do. I doubt that you would welcome your child behaving in this manner.

If you have an older dog then it will more than likely have settled down and between you there will be an acceptance of rules and regulations and a rapport that will enable you to decipher his attitude when the baby arrives. However, few can be prepared for the jealousy that may occur or how it can manifest. A dog can be jealous of the baby, or it can be protective of the baby and jealous of the midwife or doctor, it can even be jealous of one or both parents when they are nursing the baby. A dog can suddenly begin to do unpredictable things just to gain attention, chasing birds, watching television, stalking a cat – virtually anything that gains a small amount of attention one day can become a major performance the next. Most of these possible scenarios will only manifest if the dog has been allowed to believe he has some control over his human 'pack'. There is no room for an extra chief especially when a child is on the way, so if you can see any flaws in your dog's manners then the time has come to reinstate yourself as pack leader. This needs to be addressed as quickly as possible and before the new arrival.

Dogs and Children Are Not the Same

It may seem an obvious conclusion that dogs and children are not the same but actually acknowledging that they have different needs is not always so obvious. They do both need to acquire a solid foundation of good manners, house rules, a good education and strong dependable leadership. But they have different rules of hygiene, they play different games for different reasons and they speak different languages. It is worth remembering that no matter how much you love your dog it is never going to eat with a knife and fork, it will not use and flush the loo and as much as it may bark at a telephone it is never going to telephone a friend.

If this seems to be pointing out the obvious, let us look at the less obvious. A dog does not *need* toys – it is perfectly capable of finding something in the garden to amuse itself, and a bone will keep it occupied for hours, as it would in the wild. If your dog does have toys how are you going to explain that one ball is for him and the other for your child? How are you going to make it clear that the dog and child may play with toys that look alike but your child cannot chew the bone? How are you going to deal with the situation that can arise when a dog decides that the toys in the house have always been his so he takes your child's toys? What will you do when your dog grabs a baby's rattle or squeaky toy and even worse becomes angry when the baby cries?

Think very carefully about how you have been treating your dog, for if there is the slightest element of a child substitute in your behaviour towards him now this will change when a child arrives on

PREPARING THE WAY

This is a scene that can lead to a disaster or can be a special moment in time. If Tessa were a bad-mannered or jealous dog this could be an accident waiting to happen, but Kara is calm, relaxed and in control whilst allowing *Tessa to share a moment with baby Jamie.*

the scene. I love my dogs and they share my life and my home but they are my dogs, and my kids are my kids. A dog will find it very hard to accept that it has been the baby of the family and suddenly a squealing, crying, strange smelling miniature human begins to steal its thunder. If you want your dog to accept your child you must make sure it knows its own worth as a dog, understands its place in your pack, respects your rules and has a place of its own where it can retreat in peace.

Do not encourage your dog to take or beg for titbits and if you have been using this form of training I strongly recommend you throw every dog treat and titbit in the rubbish bin. What is in your hand as a titbit to be taken by permission is an open invitation to steal when it is in a child's hand. If a dog has been taught not to expect food as a titbit it will be relatively easy to teach it not to pester children for food. At no time should there be food sharing and a dog should not be allowed to lick faces or hands of children; what is hygienic for a dog is not hygienic for a human.

If your dog pulls on the lead, how are you going to manage pushing a pram and taking the dog for a walk at the same time? Or will the dog have to stay behind

PREPARING THE WAY

Tessa shows no jealousy and is gentle. Here she is showing concern for Jamie and her owner is keeping an eye on her whilst a photograph is taken to show, by the size ratio, how much damage could be done were Tessa unattended and inclined to jealousy. Even a small dog jumping in a pram can cause a lot of damage. Dogs who are allowed to investigate prams unattended may also be attracted to the smell of food on a baby. Never leave a dog and a baby unattended, not even for a second.

because it is bad-mannered on the lead? If your dog is used to travelling on the back seat of your car what will happen when there is a carry-cot or baby seat there? Teach your dog to travel quietly in the back of an estate car and behind a dog guard before the baby arrives not afterwards. If you do not have an estate car but have always taken the dog out in the car with you what is going to happen when there is no room for him? If your dog barks in the car address the problem sooner rather than later for just as the scream of a child can upset a dog so can a sudden loud bark frighten a baby or toddler; early experiences such as these can cause nervousness later.

We are human, we all make mistakes so it is important that every possible problem that may arise is tackled before it appears, prevention being better than cure. If every effort is made to ensure that as few mistakes as possible occur then the chances of a problem dog, hurt child and heartache are very slender.

PREPARING THE WAY

Chapter Summary

If you are bringing a dog into your family, make every effort to ensure that it has a good temperament but remember the nicest of dogs can make mistakes if they are not educated. If you have a dog and are expecting a baby, it is unfair to expect your dog to fit into a new routine *after* the baby is born. Begin to prepare him and his routine as soon as possible. Dogs and children have different hygiene requirements and different eating and playing habits, so do not encourage them to share toys and food.

Make sure your dog is well-mannered before your baby arrives and similarly make sure your children are well-mannered before you bring a new dog into your family.

CHAPTER 4

AVOIDING JEALOUSY

Jealousy quite often sneaks up and we are not even aware of it, or sometimes there has been a niggling suspicion but we think things will work out. This is a risk that cannot be taken. Jealousy brings out the worst in humans so do not expect dogs to be any different and don't be surprised if the cause of the jealousy is a member of the family or the latter may even *be* the jealous party.

Shall we sort the humans out first? It is not a regular occurrence but it does happen, and usually with the intention of being noticed or making a point and not of getting the dog into trouble. We've all heard the saying, 'my partner doesn't understand me', well if one member of the family understands the dog and gets on with it better than the others the relationship can begin a downhill slide. To begin with the dog will respond better for that person (who could be a child) and will do more for them; the other family members then react adversely toward the dog. This kind of jealousy, and it *is* jealousy, for each member of the family really wants the dog to accept them in the same way as the 'chosen one', will cause confusion in a young dog, but an older dog will learn how to take advantage. The confusion for the younger dog is caused because each person will endeavour to teach the dog something 'special' or maybe take it on a walk and try to train it to respond to them by food or even harsh words.

Adults cannot afford to indulge in this kind of 'game playing' if they are to gain their dog's respect but it is easily done. Let us look at an example; a new baby is born and mum is occupied, dad takes the dog for an evening walk partly because it needs exercise and partly because he is at a loose end for an hour. Prior to the new arrival the mum exercised the dog and he commanded most of her time, but now dad is lost and a bit unsure and spends a lot of time talking to the dog. The dog will begin to change allegiance, mum is put out that the dog no longer does as she says but leans to dad, and dad encourages it because he now has an ally. The dog becomes jealous when dad gives attention to the baby, mum begins to lose patience with the dog and suddenly the situation is out of hand. This situation creeps up slowly but will take a long time to sort out.

Rivalry in Children

Quite often if more than one child is involved, a dog will respond better for one than another. Once again friction begins, number one child can take the dog for a walk and can make it behave, number two child (probably younger) has to tag on at the back or not go at all. Of course number one child likes this feeling of power so demonstrates it and maybe even keeps

AVOIDING JEALOUSY

reminding number two that they are lower in ranking. Parents, where are you? If this happens, and continues to happen, number two may try to make the dog do something it doesn't like and could get bitten, or they could begin to bully the dog if it does not try to defend itself. Either way the dog will be the loser. If one child is more capable than the other, then they are the obvious choice for being in control of the dog but rather than allow that child to preside over the other, encourage an interaction where the proficient child helps their sibling to gain control of the dog.

Another volatile situation can arise if the elder child wants to try their hand at entering some competitions with the dog. If not handled correctly the younger child will feel left out and will be openly delighted if the aspirations for winning trophies end in disaster, but if accolades are imminent then the dog may just become a target for jealous anger. This scenario can also tempt parents into being a little hasty in agreeing to something they have not properly thought through and before they know it they are looking for a second dog. Fine, if this is a family decision that has been on the cards for a long time and has been made after much forethought. But believe me I have had a lot of families come to me with a problem because they have bought a second dog without careful consideration of all the consequences. If child number two is not considered capable of handling dog number one then parents will choose a smaller second dog, but what happens in a year's time when this child wants to compete but the dog doesn't? Once again a time for diplomacy, tact and encouraging the elder child to be responsible in their dealings with both dog and sibling and

If you already have a dog and are starting a family it is important that you prepare your dog before the baby arrives and not after. Tessa knows how to behave so Kara is able to take her for a walk without being pulled. This kind of training also means that Tessa will not be a nuisance when there is a pram to push.

to give the younger child a responsible 'cheer leader' position. It's all to do with teamwork.

When the Dog Came First

Well, if he was there before the baby arrived and has had lots of attention and been in control of most of the leisure time you can't blame him for not sharing your

AVOIDING JEALOUSY

enthusiasm over the new baby. In fact if you put yourself in his paws you would probably be tempted to pinch the teddy, hide the dummy and wee on the baby mat. But of course you knew the baby was due to arrive, and you can talk about any anxieties but if poor old Fido is demoted without any warning, you may expect insubordination.

It is important to change your dog's routine in plenty of time before a baby arrives so he has something familiar to fall back on when the home is disrupted. If a dog is not handled with a gentle firmness and made to understand that although loved to bits it is not in charge it will believe it has the right to make decisions. The leader is the decision-maker and if he has been allowed to be in charge then how can he be wrong if he makes decisions? You must always try to understand this and remember it when your dog does something that you believe to be wrong, for he will believe it to be right or else he would not have done it! He may look forlorn and he may look apologetic, he may even look frightened or worried but this will be because you are clearly annoyed and he will not really know why you are suddenly displeased at a decision he had every right to make. If he is jealous of the baby he will feel the need to try and get your attention, if this fails he will feel the need to turn his attention to the baby and its belongings. If he is a well-mannered, well-trained dog he will want to do these things but he will refrain out of respect for his pack leader, although he will be hurt and confused. If he is not a well-mannered dog and does not respect you as the leader he will see himself as being in control and will therefore attempt to deal with the situation as he feels fit. However if he has been prepared, is well-mannered and respects your pack rules he will be happy to wait for your attention. If you have handled the situation correctly he will not feel threatened and he will be confident that he is still a very important part of your life, even though a new pack baby has just superseded him in rank.

If you undertook the responsibility of a dog after you became a couple, but before the baby was born, it is probable that the dog has received a lot of attention as we have already mentioned. However, if the dog belonged to one partner previously it may have already shown a tendency towards jealousy. If a dog has spent its formative years with one person it can feel left out, jealous or even protective to that person when they take a partner into their lives. Once again the humans know exactly what they are doing but the dog has no idea until suddenly it is 'sharing' its owner with someone else. If the dog is not particularly well mannered problems may arise immediately or they may just fester until something provokes a jealous outburst and this could well be the arrival of a new baby.

If your dog is advanced in years when a baby arrives on the scene you will need to be sympathetic to its needs as an elderly dog, as well as to the fact that it may not be either practicable or fair to remove it from all that is familiar and safe. If it has always spent its days in the kitchen and its evenings in the living room it will neither understand nor appreciate being moved to the garden during the day and confined to the kitchen by night. You will need to make allowances; the dog will have had a revered position in your life and will need to feel safe and not threatened by the new arrival.

AVOIDING JEALOUSY

Puppies playing together will play fight and nip each other; this is natural interaction as littermates and is acceptable behaviour within the litter as they are learning how to look after themselves in later life.

It may seem harmless when a small puppy tugs at a child's leg with its teeth but it is treating the child like a littermate and this means that it believes it is acceptable to use its teeth.

Sibling Rivalry

It is not unusual for rivalry and jealousy to be seen when a group of children or brothers and sisters are playing together, it may be short-lived or it may end in a free for all. This can be the most dangerous kind of jealousy if a dog is included in the 'gang'. It may seem harmless for a dog to be included as 'one of the kids', it may even be considered beneficial if there is a protective side to the dog's nature, but dogs and children play differently. Your dog is not a littermate to your children, it is not equal to them and your children should be well versed in how to handle and

AVOIDING JEALOUSY

control the family dog. If not, and there is a scuffle, the dog may feel entitled to join in, but he will scuffle with his teeth. If there is a race and children and dog are competing for leadership, just as one child may push another, a dog may nip the children's legs to prevent them from winning. Children and dogs can play together but never as littermates and we will deal with how to make sure your children are in control in a later chapter.

Two Dogs

Until now we have only dealt with one dog in the family and with just one dog we have seen how problems can occur. If there are two dogs any problems will not only be doubled they will be more difficult to resolve. If the two dogs are well behaved and good-mannered and you not only have control of them but you also have their respect there should be no reason for any

What may seem harmless in a puppy is not so harmless in an adult dog. Stephanie and Franco are playing, but children and dogs have different ideas when it comes to games and Franco is using methods of interaction he would use on another dog.

How a dog behaves with one child it will apply in its behaviour with other children. Imagine the consequences if a dog played in this manner with a small child, and to a dog this is only playing!

problems to occur. However in many cases, particularly when the dogs are of the same or a similar age, their behaviour may leave much to be desired. Dogs speak the same language as each other and they understand each other, so whilst their owners are struggling to find some form of communication in order to train them the dogs have already made their own rules. If you can picture two strong, fit, healthy dogs playing together with one small, vulnerable child you will realize that it would only take a feeling of displeasure for the dogs to play dominantly. If jealousy then creeps into this game, maybe over a toy, the dogs can team up together and become bullies, and the child is going to be their target.

One of the most natural and excusable reasons for a dog to be protective or jealous is a bitch nursing a litter of puppies. Few families will ever be in that situation but no one can blame a mum for protecting her litter, particularly from children who will be inquisitive and intrusive. I never advise anyone to breed with their dog unless they know exactly what they are doing and when children are involved it can be a volatile situation. However placid a dog may be it can change when hormones and motherhood are involved, and the best behaved children can be difficult to restrain when they see a litter of newborn puppies.

No specific breed or dog of any particular size will behave any differently. If a dog is not educated correctly it will not respect children and no child of any age can be excused for mistreating or failing to understand a dog. Neither child nor dog will be to blame if there is an accident but both will suffer and the blame will rest on the adults. There are rare cases when a dog has, seemingly, attacked a child without any justifiable provocation but even in those cases an insight into the dog's history would probably show that it has suffered at some time in its life from either a child or an adult. Even if the dog has no apparent reason someone somewhere has failed to educate it properly.

Small dogs are just as capable of jealousy as large dogs and although they are not as strong and may not be capable of bowling a child over they can still scar a child both mentally and physically. Rules are rules and dogs recognize and appreciate a good strong pack leader. Just as children respect parental guidance so will a dog respect its leader. They may not always agree with you and they may not always like you for insisting that the rules are adhered to but they will have a foundation of discipline to understand and to abide by, and if you are strong they will accept your decisions. If you have either a child or a dog you must be the decision-maker, the one who is responsible and protective. If you have both a child and a dog you have to work twice as hard. If you have a dog and more than one child you will have to work very hard to make sure that they all understand the rules and their place in the ranking. Think very carefully before you now add another dog for if you are struggling to keep at the head of the pack with only one dog you will surely be demoted if you increase it to two.

Encourage Respect and Avoid Jealousy

It is important to encourage and nurture respect but it must be given as well as received. Your dog must respect you as the pack leader and it must respect your

AVOIDING JEALOUSY

A well-behaved dog is a joy to be with and if a child has been brought up with a responsible and caring attitude to dogs they will have fun growing and learning together. Kayleigh and Sapho take a quiet moment to enjoy each other's company.

children. It must respect your house and your garden but you must respect your dog, its privacy and its need for peace.

All dogs need their own 'space' – a quiet haven where they can rest, sleep or reflect without being disturbed. This privacy becomes even more important when there are children in the family and it is essential that it is made clear to the children that the dog's need for privacy and occasional solitude must be respected at all times. If for any reason, and it must be a good reason, this privacy or peaceful time is to be interrupted it must be done by a senior pack member, a parent. This rule is not being enforced through concern that the dog cannot be trusted with a child, for it shouldn't be in the home if it cannot be trusted, it is because this is what a dog would expect within a well-run pack.

Priorities

A dog is not a family accessory, it is a family member, albeit the lowest ranking, and as such it deserves consideration at all times. When a baby comes on the scene it is natural that your priorities will change but they must not be at the expense of the dog and its happiness. Walking the dog at night may have been an absolute 'must' whatever the weather and no matter who was visiting but suddenly it no longer seems so important, your priorities have changed. You know the dog still needs to go out but now you feel that he can make do with a few minutes in the garden and if you are busy he will be all right on his own; now your priorities have changed at his expense. You still have a responsibility to your dog and, even though you may be tired, if at all possible you still need to give the dog some 'quality time' and he still needs a life of his own and not a 'life after baby'. Discontentment can breed jealousy and a dog who is constantly being pushed aside will become discontent. Although I have advised changing your dog's routine before the baby is born, this does not mean getting him used to a lesser quality of life; it means adapting his routine and yours so everyone benefits.

AVOIDING JEALOUSY

Sharing Responsibility

There is nothing wrong with delegating but it must be done on a sharing basis. If it is likely that you may not have the time you would like in which to exercise your dog, when the baby is born consider asking a friend or family member to help. There will be plenty of willing hands to help with the baby so try to employ them occasionally for dog walking, but only when it is not practicable for you to do it. When willing babysitters are queuing up to have a cuddle or read a story, accept the offers and don't use the free time to just wash nappies; get out and have some time with your dog. You will benefit by relaxing and your dog will have some much needed quality time with you. Remember, before the baby was born you enjoyed your dog's company and although you may have changed he is still the same dog.

Throughout all stages of living with and training a dog it is necessary to 'think dog' if you are to achieve a special bond. When there are children in the family it is even more important to try to see the world, and your children, through the eyes of your dog. There will be times when, if your dog could talk, he would be running to you and asking you to make them leave him alone and there will be times when you look at a group of children playing and you know there will be tears if you don't intervene. Your dog is no exception. If the game is becoming rough or either the children or the dog are becoming hysterical then it may well end in tears. You do need to be vigilant at all times and also to try to avoid such scenes of rough play or hysteria. The best way to do this is the education of both child and dog to enable the magical bond that is possible to materialize between them making them friends rather than playmates.

Chapter Summary

Jealousy can appear in many different forms: it can be a dog jealous of a child or a toy or of sharing an owner when they have a partner.

Children can become jealous of each other if the dog responds better to one than the other. Whatever form jealousy can take it can be avoided with a little forethought. It is important to make sure that a dog is not made to feel it has been cast aside when a baby is born.

A child who can handle a dog well should be encouraged to help their sibling to understand and control the dog rather than showing off their skills.

CHAPTER 5

SAFE HAVENS

You need to provide security for both your dog and your children and quite often this is overlooked in the rush and bustle of family life, so let us take a look at why it is necessary and how best to provide it.

Always look to what is natural to a dog for guidance in how to train it and what it may expect of you. A dog in the wild would have a small secure 'den' to retire to, this would be closed on three sides and the dog would feel protected in this space as, apart from the entrance, it is closed to intruders. Try to provide your dog with a safe 'home' of its own and one that children do not have access to. A cage or plastic indoor 'kennel' is ideal with the latter being the best choice as the dog is protected from inquisitive hands. Remember, you may know that *your* children will not invade the cage but can you guarantee that someone else's child will not slip through to the dog's space undetected. Even if this child is not intrusive your dog will not know that.

If you are getting a new puppy it needs a 'den' of its own and no matter how tempting it may be for the children they must not be allowed to intrude upon the puppy's space. The first day you bring the puppy home, remember that it has just left the security of its mother and knows nothing of your family, your children or your house rules. Whatever happens on Day 1 can shape the pattern for its future so it is important that you make as few mistakes as possible. There will be a temptation for the children to want to play with the puppy on the first day; this is not harmful as puppies benefit from engaging in mild interaction with all members of the family. However, it must be remembered that whilst it is playing it is not learning anything about its new home or your 'pack' rules and it also needs time to settle in and get used to its surroundings.

I am sure that you will be keen for your children to be actively involved in the puppy's development, but if they are only young I would suggest you consider collecting the puppy when they are either in bed or visiting relatives or friends. If you have only one child there will not be the problem of one competing against the other for the puppy's attention. Similarly if you have older children they should be more responsive to the puppy's need for peace and the opportunity to settle in. It is your responsibility to decide on which course of action to take but do consider first and foremost the needs of the puppy. Try to imagine your child at a very early age suddenly being taken into a crowded room full of strangers and immediately being surrounded by them. It can be overpowering, it can be frightening or it can be so exciting that he or she becomes almost hysterical. In other words you don't know how your puppy will react but none of the above are desirable reactions the first time it enters your home.

A dog needs a safe haven of its own where it can retire to and know it will be left in peace. If it is a dog bed make sure it is situated in a quiet corner. There are many different crates, boxes and cages to choose from but remember small fingers should not be allowed to pry into cages.

The Older or Rescue Dog

I am using these terms loosely to describe a dog that is a part of your family before a child is born and a dog brought into the family that is no longer a puppy. Throughout the remainder of this book I will try to give examples of the different ages or types of dog in the family in order to cover as many different scenarios as possible. In most cases, however, we will be reaffirming the basic rules that should apply to all dogs regardless of age, breed or size.

The dog who is an established member of the family may already be used to being in a 'cage' – if not, consider trying to introduce him to one. Your dog may have a strong aversion to going in a cage although most dogs will willingly accept this 'new' home if they are introduced to it sympathetically. If your dog is a rescue then you really do need to provide an indoor 'kennel' and you do need to make sure that it is settled before the children meet it. Once again I would like to repeat the dictum 'think before you act' when it comes to choosing a dog, for you must be absolutely certain that a rescue dog is not coming to you with a dark side to its nature when you have children. Sorry, but both dog and children deserve your commitment and you cannot commit yourself to a dog that could pose a threat to your children.

We have now established that whatever age your dog is, it needs a 'home' of its own within your home. This 'home' belongs to your dog and although many will say to the contrary, that if the dog does not own its bed then it will not bite a child who enters it, I strongly disagree. A dog needs a safe haven and if it has been made to accept people standing in its bed or claiming it in any other way then it no longer has a safe retreat of its own. If there is a danger of a dog biting there is a serious problem and if children cannot be trusted to respect the dog there is an added problem. However, if a dog is well-mannered and understands its place in the pack it should not even consider biting a child, for this reason you must make sure

SAFE HAVENS

A well-mannered dog brought up to respect leadership and all members of the leader's pack will not nip or bite a child invading its private space, it will endeavour to find another quiet corner to retreat to. However, a pack leader should never allow a member of the pack to be harassed – you must protect your dog's privacy and insist that your children do likewise.

your children are responsible dog owners and do not prey on a well-mannered dog's vulnerability. My dogs always had their own 'bed' and woe betide any child, mine or otherwise, who tried to get in that bed, regardless of whether the dog was occupying it or not. In fact they were told not to go near the bed unless they were being constructive and cleaning it whilst it was empty! If there is a danger that your dog may bite your, or anyone else's, children if they were to go in or near its 'bed' then the dog does not have a place in your home. A well-mannered, well-educated dog will not bite a child who enters its bed. It will approach its pack leader for assistance in regaining its private 'space'; if you (the pack leader) are not available it will remove itself from the situation and await your return to allow you to handle the problem. In fact it may just decide to invade your space and lodge on the settee until his own 'home' is vacated. However, no dog should be put in a position of feeling threatened, and children can often be overpowering and inconsiderate of a dog's vulnerability. A dog cannot tell someone to leave it alone and in canine language a growl is as good as a rebuff and if the growl is ignored it may be followed by a nip. In either case the dog will be considered 'unsafe' when in actual fact it was just tired, wanted to be left alone and could think of no other way of telling the child to go away.

The education of children regarding your dog's privacy is as important as the education of the dog. From tot to teenager there is no excuse for rules not being upheld. Children will be told not to touch the fire as they will get burnt; not to go into cupboards where poisonous substances are kept; not to go out of the garden because of road traffic. These rules are made and vigilantly upheld for the safety of the child so why should it be difficult to add an extra one? That it is unfair to go near the dog's bed.

This rule must be one of the first ones to be taught to young children. It is a rule they must grow up with and one they must ensure all their friends understand. As a child matures, rules become more negotiable – for example, a family rule may be that a child never takes the last biscuit from a plate. As the child develops he will begin to understand the reason for the rule and therefore will be able to judge by circumstance. If a plate of biscuits has been put on the table for visitors then it could be considered bad-mannered for the child to take more than one biscuit, never mind the last one. Or it may be the last biscuit on the plate, but there are plenty more in the tin and no visitors in the house, in which case it could be perfectly acceptable for the child to eat that biscuit. This child is doing what I call 'living in the grey area' and as such will be perfectly able to work out when it is acceptable to approach the dog's personal space, its bed, and when to leave it alone. But if a child is not taught the first principle of good manners it will never be able to distinguish between living in the grey area or being badly behaved. These rules also apply to dogs. If your dog has not been made to understand that it does not own your house, that it must ask for permission and not take for granted that it can do as it pleases when it pleases, it will be a bad mannered dog.

Your dog needs a safe haven and it must respect your home. It is very difficult to get a dog to respect either you or your home if you negotiate or wait until it is settled in. It is a big mistake to believe you should begin teaching good manners after the dog has settled in, for by that time it will have already decided that you are not in control, you will not be the pack leader. Its natural instinct will have told it to expect rules and regulations from a new pack leader. After all, it is what we expect when we enter a 'new' area, be it a job, a country, a school or any other situation that has a governing body. In your home you are the governing body so you must make the rules clear as soon as possible in order for your dog to understand who is in control.

If you have a cage for your dog or puppy, always make it wait for a second after opening the door before allowing it out into your 'home'. This will establish in the dog's mind that you control the area outside its cage and it must not take liberties with this space. Children love responsibility so don't always rush to attend to the dog yourself or turn a blind eye to the fact that when they let the dog out they do not 'invite' it out, preferring instead to allow it to rush out and take over. Take time to explain to them the correct procedure, why it must be used and why it is important. If children think this method is just a form of training they may well choose to ignore it. If it is impressed upon them that the dog's whole future with you is dependent on it always displaying good manners and that they must play an integral part in the dog's education, they will take on the responsibility with pride. If the children concerned are too young to take this on board, then they are also too young to be allowed to go near the dog's cage or to let it out.

If your dog is in a bed you must try to ensure this bed is in a place in the house where it can be considered, by the dog, to be relatively safe from intrusion, and once again it is not a play bed for a child. It is the one place the dog can go to get out of the way; with this bed it can make a statement, 'leave me alone, please'. A dog must always be able to retreat to its bed with the confidence that it will be left alone.

A Child-free Zone

This is vital for your dog especially if younger children are involved. However, even when the children concerned are more mature and totally 'dog aware' their friends may not be. It must also be borne in mind that although your dog may adore every member of your family, it does not necessarily mean that it will automatically adore everyone else it meets. Like us, dogs have preferences and it may just happen that your son or daughter's best friend could be the one person your dog chooses to take an instant dislike to. Trying to force your dog to accept someone will usually only exacerbate the situation and make your dog even more antagonistic. In time it may come to accept this person but they rarely change their minds from their first instinct. This isn't a problem unless you make it one, but without a 'child-free' zone it will be difficult to cope with. You will need to respect the fact that your dog does not want to interact with this person and allow it to go to its own 'child-free' area where it can relax, chew a bone, play or snooze peacefully.

The dog's bed needs to be away from the hustle and bustle of everyday life, in a utility room or small hallway or, if these areas are where people pass through to enter the house, a spare room or the kitchen, provided it is not a thoroughfare. If there is going to be a lot of human activity such as a party, make sure the bed is out of the way, that no one is tempted to go near it and that your own family will protect its privacy. If the children are small the dog needs to be in a separate part of the house. Some dogs will interact with other children, some won't but you can never be sure how the children will react to the dog. You are responsible for the welfare of all under your roof and my advice to anyone with a dog and other people's children is to keep them apart. A big dog can make children nervous and this can spark a reciprocal feeling of uncertainty in the dog, a small dog can have the opposite effect and children may want to carry it around like a teddy bear. I cannot stress enough that a dog's teeth cause damage whether it is a small dog or a large one and whether it is a bite or an excited nip. Once a dog has caused pain (no matter how mild) that has induced a scream from a child, the consequences can quickly spiral out of control.

If the children in the family are young, for example, you have a baby or toddler and you have an established dog, there must be a totally child-free area for that dog. It is the responsibility of all parents to ensure that their children do not enter the dog-free zone until they are of an age to understand the dog and are able to learn how to handle it correctly. If this is in a

SAFE HAVENS

Few dogs can differentiate between adults and children when they are playing, especially when they are excited. This dog is used to jumping up and trying to 'wrestle' a stick from its owner. They both enjoy the game and neither of them lose control or play too energetically for each other.

The same dog jumping up at a child can cause a problem; if this dog jumps as enthusiastically for the ball as he does for the stick he could harm a small child. Note the size of the ball in the child's hand.

utility area, it will not be difficult to enforce. However, if the dog's bed is in the kitchen, it will not only be difficult but also there may be times when the dog is subjected to harassment from a child when the parents' attention is temporarily diverted.

It is most important that your dog has its own place in the garden. This could be a converted garden shed, a custom-built dog run or simply a fenced-off area with a draught-proof kennel. There are several reasons contributing to the importance of this area. If your dog has the freedom of the entire garden to patrol, as and when he wants, he will consider the garden one of his possessions which means, in his mind, that he will be entitled to behave in this area as he pleases. Problems can arise in this situation with dogs regardless of whether there are children in the family or not. The dog becomes protective of the garden barking at passers-by and eventually he may take an aversion to a visitor in the garden, which could lead to a show of aggression. This is not the dog's fault – it is the fault of the owner who unwittingly has given the dog the garden but does not

SAFE HAVENS

The forward thrust of the dog's legs could push over a small child and the mouth closing on a small ball could nip a hand. This child is used to the dog and her body language is relaxed but a different child unused to dogs, and wielding a ball, could instigate a similar reaction from the dog with serious consequences.

like the outcome when he begins to admit only those he chooses. Now imagine this same scenario but with children involved. They may play a game the dog doesn't like, they may have a friend the dog doesn't like, they may even try to play a game with the dog when it wants to rest. The dog will not believe that it is doing anything wrong if it nips or even bites the children involved because in his eyes he is in control. It will not make any difference if the dog is perfectly well-behaved elsewhere for if you have given him the garden he is free to do as he pleases in it. A group of children are more likely to incite a dog to misbehave than just one child as there will be an element of excitement in the group play. However, a child on its own can displease the dog who thinks it owns the garden and will therefore be vulnerable. This situation will not arise if the dog has his own area in the garden where children do not go.

Another reason for having a segregated area for your dog is the opportunity to keep reminding him who owns what. You allow your dog into the main garden from the house and from his pen at your invitation and you make him wait a second after you have opened his pen door to enforce the rule of 'you do not enter my space uninvited'. Simply translated, if you allow your dog to run into the garden as soon as you open the door he will associate the door with freedom, whereas if you make him wait a second *you* are giving him his freedom. He will learn to respect you as the leader who provides, makes decisions and allows him to have free time.

If you have a child-free area in the garden it can be used whenever the need arises to remove your dog from a situation. It could be a children's party, a time when a baby or toddler needs undivided attention, or simply to allow him a chance to be a dog in his own surroundings and without fear of interruption.

Your dog's cage or bed and its pen in the garden are there for his protection and safety. This doesn't mean we are presuming that children are going to molest him; it means he needs to know that he has somewhere he can retire to when he feels the need to be on his own.

SAFE HAVENS

When he enters those areas he is asking to be left alone, he will also know that if the occasion should arise when other children are present and he feels threatened by them he can remove himself from the situation and know he will not be followed. It is because this kind of security is important to your dog that you must make sure that all members of the family respect your dog's privacy and this includes children, for they are never too young to learn. Just as you want your dog to respect you, it needs you to respect it. If it knows that it will not be harassed when it is in its bed or pen should the need arise for you to enter its space, it will never question or resent you. It is no different from teenagers having their own room; they need to know you are not going to be bursting in whenever you feel like it. They need their privacy to be respected but a knock on the door to let them know you are entering is both courteous and acceptable.

Before closing the subject of a child-free zone, the size and breed of dog will dictate to a certain degree how you organize this area. If you have a large dog it will benefit from an outside area of its own and certainly should not have unsupervised access to small children. A nasty accident can occur when the nicest of dogs accidentally knocks over a child, and this does happen. A medium-sized dog will also benefit from an outside play area. Dogs need to have access to fresh air and nature but you must control it. A small breed of dog will still need to be able to sample the delights of its own 'little bit of paradise' within your garden but some small dogs, particularly toy breeds, may not appreciate being outside too long. However, toy breeds often have access to parts of a house or furniture that a larger breed of dog would not be allowed to use. These smaller dogs will often be quite happy to spend most of the day on your bed. They are often bodily cleaner than larger dogs as they are not usually given to racing through long grass and mud and are unlikely to pull the wardrobe over and tip the bed upside down. Even the smallest breeds have teeth, however, and are perfectly capable of losing their temper and using them if provoked. The same rules of making sure that the dog learns to respect your home and the people in it must apply. If you are happy for your dog to spend time on your bed away from the children it is only *borrowing* the bed – it does not own it.

A Dog-free Zone

This area is vitally important for it not only provides security and hygiene for children but it gives the dog clear rules. There is nothing more confusing for a dog than for the rules to keep changing; rules are to help him understand how to behave in your house so make them simple to understand and try to stick to them.

If you have a young child, toddler or a baby you will doubtless have an area or a room with toys, games and maybe a children's playpen. No dog, large or small, should be allowed into this area. Dogs are wonderful companions, they are faithful, they are loyal, they can be friends, guardians and an asset to a family but they also eat disgusting things! They should not be allowed to lick children, to mouth their toys or to be near their food. You need an area where toys can be on the floor, children can play with each other and food can be eaten and your dog knows it should not enter that area. If you are fortunate in having a play room it will be simple to keep your dog out of that room.

SAFE HAVENS

Do not allow your dog access to children's food and do not encourage any 'food sharing'. Copper sees no problem in helping himself to Chloe's ice cream but who is going to do the explaining when Copper pinches an ice cream from a small child? In Copper's eyes he will have done nothing wrong!

Young children and toddlers will often be playing in the main rooms of the house so it is important you begin as you mean to go on. Small children are usually in bed early so the dog could be in one of his 'child free' areas during the day and then be allowed in the main rooms at night when the toys are away. Or if you have a large room, the children's toys and play area can be in one corner or section of the room that your dog is not allowed to go into. But you will have to make your dog aware of the fact that he is not allowed in this particular area and he must also be taught not to go near the children when they are eating. This can be a tall order for many dogs as it can not only be a temptation for them when food is in a child's hand but it can be an incentive for jealousy when they are not allowed near it. Until the time of day when you are able to spend some quality time with your dog, or your child is not eating and has no residue of food on face and fingers, he is better in his own quarters.

In the garden you have already prepared for some segregation by providing a 'child-free' area. However you still need a part of the garden where children can play without the risk of treading or falling in something not very pleasant. Somewhere they can throw a ball, sit quietly (does that ever happen?) or have a friendly play fight without a dog bursting in demanding attention and interacting with them. As much as it may be a part of the plan for the dog to be able play ball with them it must not be allowed to presume that it will always be a part of whatever they are doing. This kind of presumption can lead to barking and whining when it is not included, and to jealousy or possessiveness if other children are included in the games, for example a party or gathering of school friends.

Zones Are Not Excuses

The purpose of child- and dog-free zones are to enable the dog to have some security and peace and for children to be able to play without any risk to hygiene or an

SAFE HAVENS

Think carefully before you provide a ball for your children and dog to play with. The child's hand round the small ball on the left could be accidentally nipped by an enthusiastic dog. The larger ball on the right is a better size for a small dog to play with and for a small hand to hold in safety. The centre ball is the best choice as it is a soft ball, cannot be burst and a child can kick it without having to pick it up.

unprecedented accident. Zones are not a substitute for supervision or attention and neither are they a reason for not exercising the dog or giving it quality time. Providing an area for children in the garden and then leaving them unsupervised whilst the dog has potential access to this area is not the idea. The dog should know it is not allowed in the area, but it is a dog not a machine, and just as children know they should not eat sweets before a meal but cannot resist the temptation, a dog may be tempted to flout the rules. Do not ever leave a dog and children unattended; dogs can become tempted in the same way as children.

Make sure the dog is in his area and that the children will respect his space. You are not providing your dog with a pen in the garden with room to exercise to save you having to take him out for a walk. It is a place for him to go whilst you look after your baby or children. He will be equally demanding of your time after they have gone to bed and will need some of your attention. If your children are older it is your responsibility to make sure that they take seriously whatever role you have all agreed they should play. If they are supposed to exercise the dog and you are aware that they have not done so, but

Dogs need to be given rules and when they are going to be interacting with children rules must err on the side of caution. Rob has been taught never to take a ball from someone's hand. Notice how easy it would be for a dog without manners to nip the fingers holding such a small ball.

Early in the book we established that it must be a joint decision if a dog is to be included in your family. Everyone concerned must be consulted as to the breed, size and age of the dog you are about to give a home to and each member of your family must be prepared to share the responsibility of training and exercising him.

It must be made clear to children who want a dog in the family that sharing responsibility is not an option, if they want a dog they must be prepared to put in the time and effort necessary to ensure that the dog is both happy and obedient.

Teaching a dog basic good manners does not have to come under the heading of 'boring' or 'no fun'; it can be both fun and interesting and the education of the family dog should be made part of the fun time in preference to excessive ball games.

Children like responsibility and if they are made to feel they are playing an important part in the role of training their pet they will quite often make a surprisingly good job of it. They have the time and the patience adults are often short of and even from an early age they can be taught how to make sure their dog respects them.

Having ensured that the time is right to include a dog in your family and after taking every step possible to choose a breed and temperament that will complement your lifestyle and your children's ages and temperaments it is time to move on. Dogs and children must learn to respect one another and understand that they each have a different position in your family. Interaction between them is vital but it must be carried on with certain rules and children need to learn how to communicate with a dog in order to understand it, for only then can they create a respectful, magical relationship.

neither are they at home to reprimand, the dog should not be made to suffer. It is not the same situation as failing to tidy a bedroom with the job still there in the morning, the dog will still be there but he will have been 'short-changed'. It is not his fault and he should not have to go short of fun, exercise or quality time because someone failed in their responsibility or because it doesn't seem necessary when he's been out in the garden for a while.

SAFE HAVENS

Rob would not find it easy to get his teeth into this ball even if he wanted to. He will still not make any attempt to take it from my hand even if invited to do so, he may use a paw and he may use his nose but his teeth must never come into contact with the ball, and he must not try to take the ball without being given permission to do so.

Chapter Summary

If your children are young it is important to establish 'dog-free' and 'child-free' areas in your home and garden.

A dog needs a place of its own and a simple rule of asking it to wait a second before entering your home will help to mark your space to him as one he must respect.

Your dog needs a closed-in area in the garden where he can play on his own with no interference from children and this must be an area where young children do not go. This pen or enclosure also serves to teach your dog that it does not own your garden and therefore cannot take liberties with it or with any people in it.

CHAPTER 6

FIRST STEPS, FIRST WORDS

This would be a long and repetitive book if we went through every possible scenario, from the dog being in the family prior to children, a puppy with children, an older dog with children and teenagers with dogs of differing ages. Instead we will look at the foundation of training needed for children and dogs regardless of children's ages or the breed, size and age of the family dog. Once the pack positions of the family are clearly defined to the dog you can begin to teach him the rules of your home, develop his good manners and in so doing have a biddable and contented dog. However alongside this canine education must be a parallel of similar rules, pack position (in relationship to the dog) and respectful good manners toward the dog, becoming a part of everyday education for your children.

When a new dog enters your home you must go back to basic education regardless of the dog's age. The difference between a puppy or an older dog is that the latter will, hopefully, be housetrained. However knowing it must be clean in the house does not automatically mean it knows where it should go and the fact that it may have already lived in a house does not mean that the rules it is used to are ones that you will find acceptable. So on Day 1 you need to begin education regardless of age and circumstance of the dog.

In the same way, a dog needs to know where it stands in your family (pack) and the rules it must live by, and your children must know from Day 1 of the dog's arrival how you expect them to behave. It is important they know what their role in the dog's life will be and how to look after it sensibly. The importance of beginning as you mean to go on must not be overlooked. If children are allowed to be overzealous with their attention during the first few days they will either think this is acceptable behaviour and continue with it or, if the novelty wears off a little, the dog will not understand why there has been a change in their attitude. He may be relieved, in which case he could take exception if they begin to fuss him again, or he may feel rebuffed. This situation can be avoided if you begin the first steps of education on Day 1 and both dog and child, or children, will know exactly where they stand.

Education of a Dog Towards Baby or Toddler

I have mentioned in a previous chapter that bringing a puppy into a family with a baby or toddler is not to be recommended, so we will presume that we are looking at the case of a baby and a dog that has been in the family for quite some time.

FIRST STEPS, FIRST WORDS

To avoid any jealousy from the dog towards the baby, make sure that he is not asked to sit and watch while the baby gets the attention of family and visitors that has normally been reserved for him. Give him some attention before the arrival of visitors and then put him in an outside area of his own where he cannot hear too much of any excitement that may be occurring inside the house. If it is not practicable to put your dog outside at this time, for example due to the weather or the breed of dog, give him a bone, toy or something of his own to divert his attention. Provide this in his own bed and preferably in another part of the house and leave him to either play or sleep.

If it is not for too long a period of time you can leave your dog in his own area until any visitors have gone and your baby is fed. An hour is usually long enough to leave your dog without any attention as he will already be aware there is a change in the home and he may be feeling a little left out. If he is used to interacting with your visitors allow him some time with them. It is important that you can make your dog sit and stay and that any previous habits he may have developed such as rushing out to visitors and jumping up at them are cured. Ask him to wait before going into the room and then allow him to sit quietly while he is stroked and receives some attention. If he does not usually meet your visitors, do not suddenly begin to introduce him to them; wait until they have gone and give him some attention on his own.

If your dog is inquisitive towards your baby do not try to stop him but do not allow him to investigate too closely – he may not like the smell or he may decide to try to lick the baby's fingers or face. Any sudden movement from you or raised voice, although with the best of intentions, can cause him to be startled which in turn can make him nervous or resentful of your baby. Keep quiet and calm and try not to make an issue of the fact there is a change of circumstance within your family unit. If you have been educating your dog to a new routine before the baby's arrival he will already be used to spending some time in his own area. He will know that he is not to jump up at visitors and will be used to sitting quietly in a corner of the room or on a blanket of his own while you are otherwise occupied. Now instead of knitting or reading a book you will be feeding a baby but the actual routine of waiting until you invite him to come to you for attention will not be new to him.

When you are feeding or nursing your baby, take care not to rebuff your dog if he comes forward to seek attention. Speak to him kindly, give him a stroke and then ask him to sit quietly until it is his turn for your attention. He is not high ranking in your pack, he comes below your baby but he still deserves courtesy from you and the same good manners that you expect from him. Try not to brandish rattles and squeaky toys in front of him as he may think they are for a communal game and the last thing you want is for your dog to believe he can share your baby's toys. Before your baby was born, you will have been weaning your dog away from any toys he may have had that could resemble a child's toy.

If your dog is a large breed make sure he keeps his paws firmly on the floor and try to dissuade him from any pushing habits he may have developed. It may seem harmless when a dog pushes against you or pushes through a door but to a toddler it could be the difference between standing up or being pushed over. Your baby will

FIRST STEPS, FIRST WORDS

not be in a pram for very long; he or she will soon be crawling and then walking, and those first steps should be considered when you are educating your dog to its role within your pack. What is not a problem when your baby is still in your arms can become a major problem when the first faltering steps are taken.

If your dog is a small breed take care it does not try to use the empty pram as a new 'dog bed'. If it is used to sitting on the furniture make sure you do not allow it on the settee or chair you will be using when attending to your baby. Large or small breeds should not be allowed in the baby's bedroom unattended. It is not for me to make your rules but there are some general rules that need to be applied before you develop your own. My dogs would often go into the bedroom when I put my children to bed, but they knew that they were not to interfere and they would sit quietly by the door waiting for me to go back downstairs. However, my dogs never went upstairs uninvited so I knew there was no possibility of them going into the children's bedrooms without me. They also looked forward to the time in the evening when we shared some special moments together. Even washing nappies became a shared chore.

If you know you cannot make your dog

Hannah and Tessa may be the best of friends but no matter how wonderful the relationship dogs should never be allowed to lick children's hands and faces. It is unhygienic and a dog can easily nip at a small hand just to get that extra bit of food.

sit quietly whilst you tend to your baby and you know he will take advantage and go upstairs unattended then, large or small, he must wait in his own 'home' until you are ready to spend time with him. If his manners are questionable he must not be allowed upstairs until such time as your children are much older or you know he will behave. I would not recommend a large breed of dog going upstairs at all when children are small; a stairway can be dangerous if a dog is a little clumsy and accidentally pushes a child over. In-pack decisions are yours but I would not advise you to allow your dog the run of the house or upstairs. In fact a dog should only have the freedom of the house when it accepts that the house belongs to you and you have given it permission for such freedom – this is part of the basic training and education of a dog. You make your own rules and there is little point in me saying that you should never allow your dog upstairs, if this is not going to help you with your choice of rules. Your dog may have always gone upstairs and you might not want to change this, in which case you need to know how to make sure he maintains his respect for you, your home and your family, young or old. I am not dictating how it should be done; I am trying to help you understand how your dog may see life and how to create a biddable, peaceful relationship between your dog and your child, or children, as they grow together with sensible and acceptable pack/house rules.

When a baby or toddler is on the floor, keep your dog out of the room if you know you cannot make him sit still, or if your interaction with your son or daughter may instigate a jealous thought in your dog. Always 'nip a thought in the bud' before it becomes an action; if you know your dog you will also know what his intentions are. If your dog is well-behaved ask him to sit in his designated area whilst you interact with your child. Do not make the mistake of talking to your offspring in a tone of voice your dog would previously have recognized as being directed at him. Quite often people will address a dog or praise it in a tone similar to the one in which they would address a child or baby. If they then use this tone to their baby, ignoring their dog, it will be a natural reaction for the dog to harbour jealousy. Keep contact with your dog telling him that he is good and to stay where he is. If you are going to leave your youngster playing on the floor, make sure it is in an area that your dog knows he must not enter. If your dog is well mannered, gentle and curious allow him to sit by you and talk to him whilst you interact with your son or daughter but not in a dog- or child-free zone. Do not allow or encourage interaction with a small baby. In a pack only the mother will tend her offspring, if she is going to delegate, it will be to higher members in the pack than your dog will ever be in yours. He must wait until such time as your children are of an age where senior members would give him permission to interact with them to a lower serving pack member.

The Importance of 'No'

If your dog as much as looks at your child's toys issue a firm 'No', if he so much as casts a glance at your child's food he hears 'No', if he goes anywhere near the child-free zone he will receive a firm 'No' from you. Do not wait until he has licked fingers, pinched toys or entered an area in which he is not allowed. Once he has entered it, saying 'No' is too

FIRST STEPS, FIRST WORDS

The importance of 'No'. Pat has taught Copper not to try and gain his attention and to sit and wait quietly, allowing him to talk to Chloe in peace.

late, he has already done it! If this happens he is not behaving in your home as he should and he is not giving respect to your space so he must sit in his bed for a while and think about it. But did he know that he was doing wrong? If you have not made the rules clear he has nothing to think about, has he? If you are going to ask a dog to think about a disrespectful act and he doesn't understand the rule he may blame your child for a misdemeanour he doesn't recognize. Jealousy or resentment can soon creep in if you don't seek to prevent it rather than waiting for things to go wrong and then attempting a cure.

If your dog seeks to take a ball to your youngster to try to instigate a game he must understand this is a 'No', and likewise if he tries to divert your attention to him, and away from your youngster with the ball, he will hear 'No'. If he tries to enter the children's bedroom without permission, the garden area outside his pen, dig in the garden area that belongs to the family, jump in the car or go through doors before the children, he must hear a firm 'No'. Most dogs will at some time try to upstage the children, they will try to attract your attention and attempt to elevate themselves in the pack to a status above the children. Older, secure dogs will not be as concerned with attention-seeking providing they are well-mannered dogs, but all young dogs go through adolescence and will strive to prove themselves. It is up to senior pack members (the adults in the family) to make sure the adolescent dog does not lose sight of who is in control and the fact that its status in the pack is lower than the children it is seeking to upstage. One simple word 'No' taught from an early age to both dog and children can mean the difference between frustration or freedom.

Education of Baby or Toddler Towards a Dog

Neither children nor dogs are ever too young to learn and although no one is going to be teaching a baby how to handle a dog, they can begin to learn how to behave towards a dog at a very early age.

Babies will grasp things with their fingers and most babies love to tug at hair. It often hurts, and if applied to mum and dad they have a choice of stopping the pulling or allowing it with amusement. A dog does not have this choice, unless it deliberately complains about the tugging and the only way it can do this is by growling. If it tries to move away it will either be hurt or the infant will follow it.

Parents can be quite insistent with their toddlers when it comes to going too near the fire or the road, but are not always quite so determined when it comes to protecting their dog and its space. Yet by protecting the dog they are also protecting the child. Children and dogs learn the meaning of the word 'No' very quickly. If it is made clear to toddlers as soon as they are able to comprehend that they are not to pull, tug, or do anything to a dog that could cause it distress then respecting dogs will become second nature to them. There will be dogs that don't appear to mind how much a child may lean on them or try to straddle them but even if your dog genuinely doesn't object to this, it is wrong to allow a child to think this is acceptable behaviour towards dogs. A child who thinks dogs are big cuddly teddy bears and are there to be hugged may just try and hug a dog that isn't used to children. Whatever happens you can guarantee that the dog will end up in trouble and simply because a child was not educated in safe dog awareness.

So if your baby grasps a dog's hair, open the fingers and make sure it doesn't happen again. You don't want your dog thinking this tiny being is going to be a danger to him. If your toddler attempts to go near your dog's bed, its pen, its toys, food dish, bone, anything that the dog is entitled to enjoy in peace, stop the child and explain that it is a wrong thing to do as it is unfair on your dog. Always explain

Children are never too young to learn and if they have been taught to respect a dog and not to treat it as a toy they can enjoy some happy moments, but a dog must be able to trust a child not to try to hurt or annoy them. Chloe is leaning on Copper but she knows that she must not sit on a dog or push it; her interaction is gentle.

things to both dog and child; if you don't give a child a good reason why they must not do something, then they may try again when your back is turned. Explain that your dog needs its peace and it is up to all of you to look after and protect it, and that way it will be happy to be with you and will be a good friend to you all. This is not going to make your dog want to bite your child if he does encroach on his space. If you have educated your dog correctly and you have his respect he will value the protection you are offering him and will accept an invasion of privacy either as an inconvenience or a good excuse for a game. You are making sensible rules and ensuring that your child understands his part in looking after the family dog just as the dog has had to learn your pack rules. I cannot stress enough that if you really feel there is a danger your dog may bite then for both their sakes you cannot justify having dog and child under the same roof.

If you insist that your child respects the dog as a living being and one that is entitled to some peace and personal space, you will find they not only accept this responsibility but also ensure that visiting children do not harass your dog.

Squeaky toys can really upset some dogs, their hearing is delicate and they can soon get upset at constant banging, squeaking and shrieking. Small children can be very noisy and constant screaming can have an undesirable effect on a dog, possibly creating fear, anger or over-excitement, any of which are possible stimuli to a dog acting out of character. If children are going to play noisily, educate them from an early age to play such games in a dog-free area and make sure your dog is in his own area and preferably completely out of earshot.

Small children are naturally inquisitive, often pushing face and fingers into areas that are intriguing but not necessarily safe. You must make it quite clear to your child that if your dog is in its cage the bars are not for inquisitive fingers and that at no time should he push his face close to that of the dog's. Hygiene is important and a sweet-smelling child may be a temptation for the dog to lick. More importantly, a dog can find the staring eyes of a toddler at close quarters most alarming and could see a face to face with a child as a confrontation.

The Correct Approach

Never encourage your child to approach your dog directly from the front. To a dog this is a confrontational approach and it leaves it with no escape route. Your dog and child already know each other and of course you are always there to make sure that they are kind to one another, but the better the relationship they have together the more your child may be tempted to approach a strange dog. This should never happen without the owner's consent and even then extreme caution should be taken, this means approaching the dog slowly and gently from the side and without direct eye contact. It may sound complicated for a toddler to learn this but only if they have previously been allowed to approach a dog incorrectly and without care. If your child is taught only the safe approach he will not know any other method, and should he try to force himself upon a dog you will make it quite clear this is unacceptable. You may be surprised how quickly your offspring begins to educate his friends on the subject of dog awareness.

Whenever your dog and your child, or children, are together never make the mistake of treating them as equals. Your dog is not a child and as much as he is a part of your family you will never know exactly what is going on in his head. You may not notice anything different about your children but your dog will notice if there is a slightly different smell. It could be new clothes or disinfectant, it could be a cut knee or the smell of another person

FIRST STEPS, FIRST WORDS

on your child who your dog does not like. Any of these and many more can make a dog behave out of character, sometimes a dog can sense illness in a child before it becomes apparent to a human. A canine chickenpox detector is a humorous conclusion but it can be serious if your dog takes an aversion to whatever it detects and you don't notice his slightly different attitude to your offspring.

The Gentle Approach

Small children often do not realize when they are applying physical pressure and quite often they can be so taken by the feel of what is in their small grasp that they fail to see they could be causing pain. If they are nipping at a human being or pulling their hair that person can tell them to stop, but a dog is unable to make that request in a manner that is acceptable to humans. It is important that children are taught to approach all animals gently, they need to be encouraged to speak quietly to dogs and to gently stroke rather than pat. Your own dog may be patient and understanding and if he is, then all the more reason why you should make sure your children do not abuse his kindness, however, not all dogs are used to

The gentle approach is important, there is no need for young children to be rough. Even at an early age they will benefit from being taught to care. Sinead is taking Duster out for a walk in the snow. Duster does not have to go but he likes her company and is as gentle with her as she is with him. He also understands that he must look to her as a senior pack member and respect her.

children. Some dogs may be nervous around children and some may not like the noise or smell of children. Teach all members of your family that no dog should be approached without permission from its owner, no dog should be approached directly from the front and all dogs should be stroked gently. Pulling a dog's hair, no matter how gently or how innocent it may be, is not acceptable. Brandishing toys over a dog's head or throwing toys at or near a dog is not acceptable. Screaming and running around a dog is not acceptable. Trying to ride on a dog's back is not acceptable. Pulling on a dog's collar is not acceptable. Pestering a dog whilst it is trying to eat or sleep is not acceptable. The list does not end there, but I will, as I am sure my message is loud and clear. Even if your dog is willing to accept without argument any of the above, even if it appears to enjoy it, your children must not be brought up thinking that this is a normal part of child and dog interaction. Teach your children responsibility, care and gentleness first and any bonus interaction that your dog accepts must be appreciated by all, respected and not presumed by your children to be acceptable behaviour towards any other dog.

Points to Remember

Small hands can become stuck in a dog's collar and a lead wrapped around the hand of child can be dangerous if the dog on the other end of the lead suddenly decides to go for a run. Small dogs are obviously not as strong as large dogs but I remember seeing a small child proudly holding the lead of not too large a dog whilst mum was pushing a pram. The dog cannot be blamed for having a single canine thought when it set off across the road to chase a cat, dragging the screaming child after it. Fortunately there were no cars and no harm was done but it proves that even a small dog can have the strength to pull a child over if its adrenaline is working overtime. If your child wants to be responsible and 'help' to walk your dog, make sure you are holding an extra lead to enable dual control until you feel both dog and child are responding to each other.

Most children like playing with a ball and most dogs like to join in any ball games. Small children have tiny hands and if they are playing with a small ball it is all too easy for the dog to take hold of the ball and nip their fingers. Make sure the ball is large enough for the dog not to be able to get its mouth around it, a soft football is ideal, and make sure your dog knows it must always surrender the ball when told to do so.

Before your children are allowed to play ball with a dog you must teach your dog how to play without there being any danger of nipping or chasing. A dog should always drop the ball when told to do so and if you can teach your dog to retrieve a ball by 'dribbling' it with its nose then so much the better. One of my dogs knows if he is playing with children that he is not allowed to use his teeth. When the ball is thrown he catches it with his paws, if he retrieves he dribbles it back and then places his paw on the ball to prevent it rolling away. It can be part of a fun game teaching your dog how to behave with children during a ball game. Dogs only know what we teach them, so if your dog is excitable with a ball, uses its teeth and tries to tug it from your hand, who taught it to do this? It is we humans who decide

FIRST STEPS, FIRST WORDS

Small hands can get stuck in collars and a lead looped over a child's hand can cause a nasty accident if the dog makes a sudden dash in the opposite direction. Skye is small but compared to Hannah she is very strong, this picture was taken under supervision but proves how easily a child could be pulled over.

Rob knows he must not jump for the ball, not even when an adult is holding it. Making a dog wait to be given permission to play with a ball does not make a game any the less interesting and it does mean a child is not in danger of being pushed over.

how dogs play with balls so it is far better to teach them to play gently and not to be possessive.

Never encourage a dog to chase. Chasing birds in the garden, chasing after sticks, rabbits, other dogs are all instigators of problems as a dog matures. The chasing will cause excitement that in turn can lead to hysteria and the dog will lengthen the distance it is prepared to chase in order to catch its prey. If a chasing dog does manage to catch its prey you can guarantee it will use its teeth and the problems this can cause are extensive. Cats can be killed by a chasing dog; a dog can be run over and cause an accident chasing across a road; chasing bicycle wheels can cause an accident; chasing car wheels can kill a dog; chasing people running can cause a nasty bite. Any dog that has bitten will be classed as aggressive and may have to be put down. Chasing

FIRST STEPS, FIRST WORDS

When Rob has possession of the ball he knows the 'no teeth' command and will quite happily use his nose to control it and then to roll it back to his handler.

is a result of lack of discipline and rules; if a dog has been allowed to chase, or has not been taken to task over a developing chasing habit, it can lead to misery when children are involved. The dog will not find it difficult to catch the children it is chasing and will invariably nip their legs.

If your dog is in the garden and your children are running harmlessly across the lawn, the dog can appear from nowhere and cause serious damage to small limbs, not to mention the mental scars it will leave. The dog will be blamed but it will only have been acting on an impulse or habit that it has previously been allowed, or even encouraged, to indulge in. Dogs do not need to chase, and ball games do not need to stop because the dog may chase, in fact a ball game can be an excellent way of teaching your dog *not* to chase. If your dog is not 100 per cent obedient at sit and stay then ball games are out of the question. Teach him some manners first and then ask him to sit and stay whilst you gently roll the ball a few yards away. When the ball has come to rest, wait for a second and then allow him to go to it; the purpose of not sending the ball too far to begin with is to prevent the dog from tearing off at a great pace. The slower and quieter you can keep your dog the gentler he will be with children.

Many training methods employ the use of titbits. I personally do not believe in this method; I teach my dogs manners

FIRST STEPS, FIRST WORDS

Right: *This may appear like a harmless scene, a dog in the garden and a child playing. They are not playing together so where is the harm? Were Hannah to fall on Skye, taking her by surprise, the dog could not be blamed for having an instant reaction of growling or even nipping. This scene was obviously supervised but it shows how accidents can happen. Never leave a dog and a child unsupervised, no matter how reliable you may think they are.*

Below: *A child and a dog can enjoy each other's company but only with the correct education. Henry and Hector are supervised and Hector knows that he must respect Henry; he does not perceive him as a littermate and has been educated not to use his teeth on a ball without permission.*

and words for actions, I then expect them to respect my wishes out of love for me not what I may be able to offer from my pocket. If a dog is used to taking titbits as a reward for simple everyday good manners it may presume that a request to 'sit' from a small child will reap such a reward if it does as requested. This could lead to the dog almost molesting the child in search of a 'reward'. It can also lead to licking or nipping fingers putting both hygiene and safety at risk. One last word about toddlers and dogs. Do not encourage investigation of the dog bowl by the child or of the child's plate by the dog. Food from the table, titbits, licking plates and licking fingers are not advisable as, apart from it being totally unhygienic, it also places the dog and the child on the same level and this is not acceptable.

Your dog must not be allowed to perceive your children as his littermates, he is lower in pack status to them and must be encouraged to see them as human beings with the knowledge and confidence to lead him and not vice versa. A dog can always sense vulnerability and anything vulnerable it may sense in a child must guide it to protect the child and not to take control of it.

Teaching a dog its place in the pack is not difficult but it must also be combined with educating children how to be higher in status in the pack. Otherwise even the best mannered dogs may succumb to the temptation of trying to control the children rather than listening to and respecting them. Children grow quickly and they need to be taught as soon as possible how to be gentle with a dog, however no sooner have they learned the art of gentleness than they must begin to learn how to be assertive without losing that gentleness. So with toddlers and dogs under control it's time to take a look at how to teach children dog management and how to ensure that your dog responds.

Chapter Summary

No matter how patient your dog may be, it is still important to teach children to respect it. If children are not taught how to be kind and understanding to your dog, they will not know how to behave correctly when they see a strange dog, and not all dogs are used to children.

Your dog must take second place to your baby in ranking but that does not mean it should be excluded from family interaction.

Teach children and dogs the meaning of the word 'No'.

Teach your children to approach your dog from the side and not with 'face-to-face' contact. This is important for your dog and an invaluable safety precaution when your children meet other dogs.

CHAPTER 7

GAINING RESPECT

It is difficult to know where to start and when to stop when giving advice regarding children with dogs. There are many things I can advise against or encourage parents to do but it all depends on circumstance. For example, when my children were young we always had several dogs, so it would be wrong of me to say children and dogs do not mix. But there was only ever one dog they had regular contact with – Floss was the answer to every parent's dream where dogs and children are concerned. My children were very lucky, not because there were several dogs but because of Floss. Had she not been a part of our family my children would not have been able to interact with the other dogs in the same way as they did with her. However, the wonderful relationship that developed between Floss and my two children did not just happen. The *ingredients* for a wonderful relationship happened, in the respect that my children were used to animals and had been taught to respect them from a very early age plus Floss had a kind and gentle nature. Had my children not been as sensible with dogs, Floss may not have responded to them and had Floss been a less gentle dog the children may not have created an empathy with her. The foundation had already been established with two children and one dog who were all well-mannered and respectful towards one another, but this did not mean that the hard work was finished and I could just leave them to their own devices. On the contrary, I was constantly reminding all three of them that they must remember their manners and I expected, in fact I demanded, that my children did not allow Floss to be subjected to unwelcome advances from other children. Floss was a part of our family, we fed her, trained her and looked after her and she trusted us, so to abuse that trust by not considering her feelings would have made us unworthy of her loyalty. Over a period of months Floss became popular with many of my children's friends but only the ones who were prepared to treat her with gentleness and respect.

During the years that followed Floss's death many other dogs have benefited and still do from the wisdom she bestowed upon my two children. Floss was a hardworking sheepdog but kind to children, her breeding was of a gentle nature but this was not in evidence when working stubborn stock. She was willing to accept other children but only if they were gentle; if not, she would retire to her bed until the unwelcome visitors had departed. If strangers came in the yard Floss would stand between them and my children, but when family visited and were playing Floss showed no sign of possessiveness or jealousy. I also had a white sheepdog when my daughter was born and she would spend hours sitting at the side of the pram being protective but not possessive. The only time we had a problem was when the nurse visited and Lass decided that she really could not accept someone smelling so unfriendly (disinfectant) to pick my daughter up. As soon as I saw a look of distrust in my dog's eyes she was removed from the room, but I was not annoyed with her, far from it – she just hadn't quite figured out who was acceptable and who wasn't. So I am not just explaining training methods and the reasons for them at random. I have brought children up with dogs, I have dealt with dogs that like children, dogs that tolerate children and dogs that do not like children. I have learnt that making mistakes is inevitable so avoiding as many as possible is advisable, and knowing how to handle a mistake is paramount.

Usual Problems

Unfortunately there is very rarely just one problem as one invariably leads to another and when someone contacts me with a problem regarding their children and the family dog, what may have begun as a small problem has often manifested into several larger ones. There are usually three questions I ask when someone has a problem dog. Does it come back as soon as it is called, does it pull on a lead and what do you feed it on? In nearly all the cases the dog does not have an instant recall, it pulls on the lead and it is often fed on an unsuitable diet for its breed and the amount of daily exercise it receives. Many of them are showing signs of aggression, few of them have a bed or area of their own. I can remember one poor dog trying desperately to climb on my furniture to avoid the grasping hands of the little three-year-old monster who was making his life a nightmare. The dog has been smacked for growling at the child and received no protection whatsoever from the child's parents who were too busy being amused by their offspring's antics! This case was an exception as most dog owners are genuinely trying to get it right, but it needs remembering as it serves to point out that if your dog is well-mannered and a 'wild' child approaches it in the street your dog can be made nervous of children. Similarly if your child were not taught the gentle approach and met the dog from the above scenario in the street then both may suffer.

Here are some of the problems I hear: my dog will not play with my children. My dog loves my children but won't allow anyone other than family near them. My dog is good with my children but growls at other children. My dog was play fighting with my child and bit him. My children were play fighting and my dog joined in and bit one of them. My dog is good with one of my children but behaves strangely with the other. My small dog used to sleep at the foot of my child's bed but now creeps up onto the pillow during the night. My large dog has begun pushing my child to one side to get attention. My dog chases the children, rounds them up and nips them. This is only a fraction of the list I could provide but it serves to show some of the questions and problems that can arise, and if you look closely at them they are a product of lack of rules and discipline. All of them stem from the dog being promoted, albeit unwittingly, to a position in the family pack that allows it to make executive decisions. So in the eyes of the dog it is not committing a crime, it is simply acting on its own orders.

GAINING RESPECT

A dog should not be expected to play with children, it is not mandatory to want to play but a bonus. You may wish for a dog that will be happy to interact with children but all the forward planning in the world cannot make a dog's nature into something that is alien to it. This, however, does not mean your dog cannot still be a wonderful part of your family – it simply means he doesn't like children's games. He is a dog, not a toy and if he doesn't fit the criteria you had in mind for him, I'm sure you will find him an asset in other parts of your family life.

Not allowing people other than immediate family near the children is a dog being possessive and although it is not mandatory for your dog to like other children it has no right to take the law into its own paws. In both cases the dog is assuming control and making decisions that it has no right to make, although in its eyes it clearly believes it has a right to be in control.

If a dog is allowed to interact with children on a regular basis with no rules or order of ranking and if it perceives your children as its littermates it has every right to include itself in what it sees as litter fights. It will deal with siblings as it thinks fit, usually by nipping them, and in fairness to the dog it will find it quite acceptable if the child nips back, that's what littermates do!

It is not usual but it does happen that a dog will accept one child and not another. I have known cases where parents have been adamant that there has been no reason for this favouritism but in each case we have traced back to an occasion when the unpopular child has done something to alienate the dog. In one instance the child happened to be standing near a car when it backfired and the dog blamed the child for the noise.

The small dog on the bed and the large dog pushing the child are cases of failure to take forward planning into consideration when training the dog and insisting on good manners. It could just as easily be a large dog trying to take over the bed and a small one trying to push in front of the children.

Rounding children up? This remark is one of my pet hates and I find it incredible that trainers use this explanation as an excuse for a dog that clearly needs training and to people who genuinely need help in training their dogs. Study a litter of puppies playing and you will see them interacting with each other in games that are instinctively designed to teach them how to survive in later life. These games will be carried through into the adolescent pack where supervision from senior pack members will ensure that the younger generations are prepared for adulthood and sustaining the future of the pack. The puppy and adolescent dog will not interact in the same way with its mother or senior pack members as it will with its littermates and herein lies the answer to so many questions. You must make it clear to your dog that you are the pack leader and then you must make sure you establish your children as senior pack members. At no time must your dog see your children as his equal in the fields of play and interaction and you are not doing him a kindness by allowing him to believe they are littermates. Sooner or later he will do what to him is natural but to you is a threat to your child's safety. You may be hurt, confused and angry as to why your dog has behaved in a way you deem to be unacceptable but he will be just as hurt and confused when your attitude to him suddenly changes. You will not find it difficult to be stern with your dog if he threatens to bite your child, so find it within yourself sooner rather than later to be firm with him and teach him what he needs to know rather than allow him to assume a role of his own choosing.

Do Dogs Round Children Up?

Well, why would they? It is believed that if a dog's natural instinct is to herd it will automatically herd children. Most dogs will have characteristics and instincts peculiar to their breed but these do not rule their lives and they need not be a problem. Dogs only know what they are taught. If you teach your dog to use its instincts, it will; if you teach it to harness its instincts, it will. If you have a dog bred to retrieve and it retrieves endlessly, pinching other people's balls and scenting rabbits miles away, do you blame its breeding? I know of many dogs who do just that but they are not bred to do it, they are just uneducated. If you have a dog that is bred to herd and you allow it to indulge in this instinct it will probably round up the cat, the ducks in the park and it might even try to round up a budgie but, believe me, its instinct does not run to seeing children as prey.

There are conflicting opinions as to why dogs should run round children and chase them, and why it often leads to nipping. The main theory is that the dog, that will be a working breed, relates to the children as if they were sheep or cattle. I find this a strange concept as working dogs are bred and trained to herd, chasing is not acceptable and neither is random nipping – a working dog should only ever use its teeth on command. A working dog is trained to do a job that it is bred to do, if this dog is not in a working environment it should be trained to do what it is or is not needed to do in a domestic environment. Some breeds of dog are natural barkers but they will not be encouraged to bark in a companion home as it will be apparent from the start that the barking will lead to unwanted noise. Dogs that have a working instinct of any kind need to have that instinct harnessed or they will not make the companion or family dog you are seeking. It is an accident waiting to happen allowing any breed of dog to chew, destroy, chase, bark or become so excited when playing that it verges on hysteria. The dog that is undisciplined in any of the above areas is a liability if it is playing with children and regards them as littermates. A dog 'rounding' up children is doing what is natural within a puppy pack – it is interacting and assuming the role of puppy leader and, as such, it is entitled to nip. If it gets excited it will nip with intent. Small dogs will interact in a similar way, not quite so intently perhaps but often exuding more hysteria; they will also nip when they become excited. What instincts are we going to put this down to? A dog that is allowed to chase balls without any form or discipline, to chew and nip without being told that this is not acceptable and allowed to mix with children without any rules of hierarchy will eventually do something unacceptable. Please do not blame the breed of dog nor allow trainers to convince you that you have chosen the wrong breed. Blaming the breed is, in most cases, failing to accept responsibility for it. If the breed is not the one best suited to your lifestyle and you are convinced that the breed of dog is at fault you will

GAINING RESPECT

Children should not be encouraged to feed titbits to dogs but they do need to know how to approach a dog and there may be times when hand feeding is acceptable. Here Hannah can be seen offering a treat that is big enough for the dog to see.

not try to resolve the matter with conviction, and if you rehome the dog you will not train a second dog any differently. Accept any mistakes and failings and get on with making up for lost time by embarking on a sensible, no tibtbits and no concessions unless earned, training programme. If the safety of your children is at stake, keep your dog separate and try to introduce a training regime whilst you find a new home, if possible doing this yourself. Rescue establishments are for dogs that need rescuing and few can rehome a dog that is an accepted danger. You are just as well equipped to find a good home yourself and if it has to be put down it should not be after spending time in a kennels on its own with no friendly face to relate to. I am telling it as it is, not how it could be done to save personal stress. If we take a dog into our home we owe it a good life or at least honesty if we cannot cope. I must stress that many problems would not arise if greater forethought was used when choosing a dog. Very large dogs are not ideal for small children but small dogs are often not deemed energetic enough for growing children. This leaves the medium-sized dog as an ideal family first choice; not too big and not too small, but they are still dogs and need training to be respectful pack members. If your first choice of breed is a working breed and

GAINING RESPECT

Hannah has approached from the side and shows no nervousness, as she is feeding a dog that she knows is both kind and gentle. She is also being supervised as she learns how to behave sensibly with Tessa.

you are not prepared or not equipped as a family to accept this and educate it accordingly, then for the sake of your peace of mind and a dog's happiness please make a different choice. This is not failure and it is not 'second best', it is acting responsibly to ensure that you are choosing a dog that will be right for all the family and not just one person.

What Children Need To Know

If you already have a dog and you are about to start a family, of all the problems that may arise jealousy and possessiveness are probably the most traumatic to deal with. However, if you begin early education with your dog and then continue the good work with your children as they grow, the disadvantage of having to cope with any early problems can be compensated for by the fact that your children are growing up familiar with animals and how to look after them. Children who are not used to dogs need to understand what is involved in looking after a dog and to accept that they must share in the responsibility for its well-being.

Before a dog comes into your home there are many things you can teach your

GAINING RESPECT

children to prepare them for the event, in fact there are certain rules all children should be aware of regarding dogs.

How to Approach a Strange Dog

No one should ever approach a strange dog, children see dogs on the beach, in a park, tied up outside a shop and they are tempted to go and stroke them. It is paramount that children are taught that to follow this temptation is both inconsiderate and dangerous, not all dogs are used to children and dogs that are tied up are vulnerable. A dog running loose can move away from anyone it does not like, but an excited or dominant dog could choose to nip a strange child rather than run away. A tethered dog does not have the option to run, so it either has to accept children's advances, welcome or otherwise, or defend itself from the unwanted approach. Whatever happens the dog rarely wins – if it growls it will be in trouble, if it bites it is in serious trouble, if it does neither but is nervous it could be made wary of children for life. If it enjoys the attention it may approach other children expecting a game and may get hurt, not all children are nice to animals. Whatever the scenario, the dog could suffer and the dog's owner will be the one left to pick up the pieces. If the dog has bitten it may have been an

No child should approach a strange dog and a tethered dog is vulnerable. This child is approaching directly into the dog's space and the dog is making it very clear that it is not happy.

GAINING RESPECT

Look how dangerous this is. The only thing stopping the dog is the tether and the child's face is in the firing line!

aggressive dog that should not have been left unattended but it may just have been an innocent dog that simply wanted to be left alone. The consequences for the child depend on the dog's behaviour; if it accepts the advance there will be no immediate harm done but the child may approach a less friendly dog another day. If the dog is unfriendly then at best the child is frightened and at worst bitten.

The following approach applies to both adults and children. Always ask the owner before approaching the dog and never approach from the front. Approach from the side, keep the body relaxed, do not stare into the dog's eyes, move slowly but not hesitantly, allow the dog the time and opportunity to sniff, inspect and decide whether it wants any further attention. Keep a common-sense attitude, and explain to children in a way they can relate to. They would not like it if a total stranger came up to them in the street and tried to cuddle them, they would be even more upset or frightened if they were cornered, which is akin to the tethered dog. They would probably jump if someone rushed passed them so when they pass a strange dog they should always slow down and walk past. They often get excited and do things they

GAINING RESPECT

All's well that ends well, but only because this was supervised. The child is used to dogs and this dog is actually very kind but does not like a direct approach. Yes, we set this picture up but unfortunately this kind of scene does happen in real life and from the picture you can see how vulnerable both dog and child are.

to consider the dog and to try to see things from its point of view.

How to Feed a Dog

It may sound like a silly statement, but children do need to know how to look after a dog and feeding comes into general dog care so it should be part of the child/dog education programme. The dog should be asked to sit, the child approaches from the side, places the dish quietly down in front of the dog, stands back and gives him permission to eat. The child then walks away and leaves him to enjoy his meal, not forgetting to tell him he's a good dog. Parents should be supervising this and telling the dog to sit and wait, eventually the child tells the dog to sit and wait and parents should make sure that the dog does as the child says. Never allow a small child to feed a dog and when they are old enough to learn, never leave them to do it unattended. Never allow small children to give dogs titbits. When they are old enough, they should approach from the side and hold out the titbit, making sure that it is large enough for the dog to see. It is important to keep a steady hand and not to jump or tense up when the dog reaches for the titbit as this may alarm the dog, it may even think the offer of the titbit is about to be withdrawn. I am not a big believer in an ad lib supply of titbits to dogs, if you are not careful, there is a danger of becoming a human vending machine. Where children are concerned I think it is an unnecessary complication as dogs can become greedy and nippy when food is offered on a regular basis and for no apparent reason. If a dog is used to being given titbits it can hardly be blamed for taking an ice-cream out of a child's hand that appeared to be on offer.

wouldn't normally do, as do dogs, but dogs tend to nip when they are overexcited. Children often want to be left alone. They sometimes don't feel like playing. They are entitled to their thoughts, feelings and privacy and so are dogs. Children both can and will understand and relate to dogs if they are taught

GAINING RESPECT

Win is instructing her granddaughter Becky how to feed Di. Her dog is asked to wait while Becky puts down her dish of food.

Although Di's food is in front of her she is still asked to wait; this will prevent her from trying to rush to eat the food before Becky has stood up.

GAINING RESPECT

Di is given permission to eat and Becky has learnt an important lesson in how to look after a dog and she can leave Di to eat in peace.

Tug of War

This has to be a *No* as far as I am concerned. It is dangerous and can lead to aggression. Dogs should never be encouraged to use their teeth and when children are involved they should be distinctly *discouraged*. If you see your child with a lead, a stick, a toy or anything else being used as a tug of war with your dog, explain why the game has to stop. It may seem like fun to a human, especially a child, and no doubt the dog will be having tremendous fun but it has a stronger grip, a stronger instinct and a very strong bite when it gets mad or excited! A dog will soon learn to grab at the tug object and its canine puppy 'learning how to kill' game will spring to the surface of its mind. It can become obsessed with 'winning' the game and in its efforts it can bite the hand at the other end. Even if you think the game is under control and is harmless with your child and the family dog, will it be as harmless when a visiting child happens to pick up a toy and wave it in the air? Who will be blamed if the dog does what is has done previously and grabs at the 'tug' causing the child at the other end to be either frightened or bitten? When you have a dog and children in

GAINING RESPECT

Hannah-Jo is facing Ellie but both dog and child know each other and Hannah-Joe knows not to rush at or cuddle dogs. Ellie has been taught to respect children and will not try to pull anything from a child's hand.

your family you will always have to take into account other people's children, their behaviour and their attitude to dogs.

Learning lasts forever with dogs, it can also be a journey of self-discovery and a child learning to understand nature and animals is a wealthy child.

Chapter Summary

Joining in children's games is not mandatory for your dog; it does not make it any less special if it chooses to sit and watch rather than join in.

Medium-sized dogs are often the most popular size for a family dog but this size includes a lot of working breeds. You will have to learn about the breed and take care to harness its working instinct and not to encourage it. If you do not think you can give the commitment to such training then choose a less demanding breed. Dogs do not round children up as part of an instinct, it is part of sibling games. When teaching your dog and your children how to behave you will have to allow for other people's children not being as used to dogs or knowing how to behave with them.

CHAPTER 8

LIVING, LOVING AND LEARNING TOGETHER

It is not all hard work, but I would be guilty of deception if I were to say it is easy bringing children up to be responsible dog owners, and teaching dogs to respect children. I think it is important to remember that as parents and dog owners we must never take anything for granted. It is not difficult to issue instructions, however, if those instructions are not fully understood, or the importance of carrying them out correctly is not made perfectly clear, the task of sorting out the ensuing mess can be a mammoth one. Teaching older children how to look after and train a dog is no less important than teaching younger children, but sometimes older children think they already know all the answers and sometimes parents presume they may know enough. Looking after a dog and training it requires a good dose of common sense and if children are taught to be sensible and responsible and always to think before they act, they should be well on their way to building up a good relationship with the family dog.

Giving Older Children Responsibility

Children will have an idea in their own minds how they want life to be with their dog. Some of the things they envisage are not advisable, some are fine if they understand the dog and how to handle it, and some are recommended.

Before embarking on any games the dog must understand its place in your pack – it is not the leader, it is not high ranking and it does not have human littermates. Never ignore any attempt your dog makes at belittling your children's authority, dogs will try to turn a deaf ear to adults so they will most certainly try it on with children. Make sure you set some time aside each week not just to teach your children how to handle your dog but also to inculcate in your dog that it must respect your children.

If a dog ignores a child when he tries to command him, the child will either repeat the command (this will lower his credibility of leadership in the dog's eyes), try to manhandle the dog to do his bidding or he will allow the dog to flaunt flagrant disobedience by not addressing the issue. Always back your child up if your dog ignores him, make it quite clear to your dog that he must do as he is told. A dog that gets away with ignoring a child when the adults are present will have little respect for that child if they are on their own.

Children as well as adults must adhere to simple everyday rules of dog training although I prefer to call it common-sense

LIVING, LOVING AND LEARNING TOGETHER

When children are playing they will 'play fight'; when dogs are playing they also will 'play fight'. All breeds of dogs play in this manner and the older they are the more skilled they become at canine wrestling. Children use their hands and dogs use their teeth, for this reason they must never be allowed to combine their play fighting. Dogs must not think of children as littermates, for if they do they will think that this kind of playing is acceptable.

good manners. Quite a lot of training is for something specific and extra to normal everyday activities – for example, adults and children can be training for a specific type of job, career, sporting activity but outside this training they should still retain good manners. Individuals' ideas of good manners may differ slightly but there are certain universal manners that are (or should) be taught to children in order for them to mature into polite, acceptable adults. Dogs need to be given a similar 'code of ethics' and if you think of educating your dog in the same way as parenting a child the parallels are remarkably similar, making it easier to understand and execute.

Ten Commandments for Your Dog

You will not pull on a lead.
You will not demand attention when we are busy.
You will not push in front going through doors.
You will not ignore us when we call you.

LIVING, LOVING AND LEARNING TOGETHER

You will not pull, tug or try to take anything we are holding.
You will not lick children's hands and faces.
You will not take any food that does not belong to you.
You will not try to take a ball or any other object from a child's hand.
You will not show any sign of aggression to a child.
You will not try to behave as a littermate to a child.

Ten Commandments for Your Children

You will always treat your dog with respect.
You will discourage your dog from pulling or tugging anything from your hand.
You will make sure that your dog does not pull on a lead.
You will give your dog regular, small 'good manners' training sessions to ensure that he listens to you.
You will insist that other children respect your dog.
You will not continue to play with your dog until he becomes over tired or over excited.
You will respect your dog's need to have a peaceful place of his own.
You will not do anything to cause your dog distress or discomfort.
You will not allow your dog to roam too far from you on a walk.
You will not allow your dog to run loose amidst strangers or unknown dogs.

These are simple rules and if you study them they are all common sense but they are also linked to each other and together they form a solid chain of interactive good manners. For example, picture a group of children all rushing through a door to play in the garden. If your dog includes himself in this group of legs, arms and giggling he has become one of the 'gang' – they are all buddies going out together. There is nothing wrong with this concept except canine buddies that consider themselves equals play fight and this is not acceptable behaviour for canine and human interaction. If your dog is taught to wait and follow he will also be waiting to be invited to follow and to be included in any games. There is a subtle difference between the two and although it may seem trivial and even a chore enforcing this rule of manners it is worth the effort, for within this rule also lies a subtle message to your dog – that is, that he is not equal to your children who are above him in pack reverence. Parents must accept the initial responsibility for employing these manners when children are young but the older child should share in this responsibility. There is no excuse for a child who is old enough to play on his own without adult supervision not to ensure that his canine friend is well-mannered. Parents make their own rules but I would advise that you make it clear to any children of whatever age (they are never too young nor too old), by saying 'If you don't make the effort you won't be allowed to enjoy the dog's company.'

If children are taught how to walk a dog correctly on a lead and are made to understand that it is not acceptable to run along a pavement as fast as possible with their dog doing an impersonation of a sled dog, they will not be in danger of losing control. If they are absorbed in a game with other children, it is not a reason to let their dog

LIVING, LOVING AND LEARNING TOGETHER

It's wonderful to have a friend to talk to and to tell a story to, even if she has to be reminded, 'Listen to me when I'm reading to you.'

children responsible tasks, within their capabilities, in the general care and well-being of your dog. Young children will realize that it is not a toy but a living being with thoughts and feelings, and older children will discover a wonderful world of natural communication.

The Green Cross Code

This is part of the essential learning curve for children but it is also invaluable for your dog. He may not know what he is looking for but he must learn to sit and wait until he is told to cross a road. This is an easy exercise for older children, who are used to going out on their own to teach a dog, and they can also have fun teaching their dog new words. For example, the dog is not allowed to cross a road or path until he hears a certain word or sound, 'cross now' sounds like one word with two syllables so it rolls off the tongue. This can be taught crossing a path in the garden so there is no danger involved. But once it is learned your dog will not rush across a road. He will go at a sensible speed and will not go without being given permission.

All training should be done for a reason and not just for the sake of it, so let us look at how the above can be implemented and prove to be a valuable lesson. You can rarely be certain when a younger child may be involved with your dog, whether a younger sibling or a visitor. If a dog has been used to crossing a road with an older child and has been allowed to run across, maybe dodging traffic, the dog will not have any 'road sense'. If a younger child has hold of the dog's lead and it dashes across the road the consequences do not

off its lead and allow him to roam free and unsupervised.

If a pet comes into the home, it should be a shared responsibility. The child who keeps forgetting to feed the pet rabbit, fails to keep it clean or spend time with it, may promise to spend every available moment with a dog but what will happen when the novelty wears off?

Responsibility is often the instigator of protective instincts – remember that first important toy, car, house? Give your

LIVING, LOVING AND LEARNING TOGETHER

When children are brought up with animals they become part of everyday life – there is no sudden novelty and no tiring of responsibility. Hannah finds neither fascination nor fear in Floyd, the pot-bellied pig, he is simply another friend to talk to.

bear thinking about. When older children share the responsibility of caring for and teaching your dog, they are also protecting younger siblings or visiting children who may not be as strong or as capable as them.

Ball Games

It would be difficult, if not impossible, to ask children not to include the family dog in ball games so it is important that they know how to play in a safe and controlled manner. To begin with, parents need to make sure that their dog is well-behaved and controllable before it is allowed to interact with children in any game. Older children are perfectly capable of training a dog but they need to follow certain guidelines. Buy them a book on training, talk to them about what you all expect from your dog, compare commands and make sure you are all using the same words. A nice collar and lead are so much more special if they choose them themselves. Encourage them to contribute a little towards the dog's keep or his extras, and perhaps to take nice photographs of special days as this all contributes towards bonding. To encourage your dog to bond with your children, ensure that they

LIVING, LOVING AND LEARNING TOGETHER

Children are going to want to play ball games but parents must make sure their dog is sufficiently well-behaved before being allowed to interact in any games. Rob is a very strong work dog but he is also kind and well-behaved, I have lost count of the number of handicapped children he has given pleasure to with his loveable antics. Rob's good manners did not just 'happen' he has been taught how to play gently and safely.

take part in any grooming, that they have the chance to put him to bed some nights, that they walk with him when you are out, rather than playing or leaving him to you. Dogs are for life, and along with the pleasurable side of owning one are the slightly less pleasant activities. Visits to the vet, exercising when the weather is cold and wet, drying him off when he is soaked through, nursing him if he is unwell, all are part and parcel of dog ownership and older children can be fully involved in all aspects.

When there is a bond of affection, good manners and respect between dog and child, 'extra curriculum' can begin. Let us assume there is one child and one dog, rather than continuously throwing a ball for the dog to fetch back it can be taught to sit and wait before retrieving the ball.

LIVING, LOVING AND LEARNING TOGETHER

Here Rob is being taught how to control the ball without using his teeth and to remove his foot when mine touches the ball.

Hide the ball and ask the dog to seek it but don't allow it to become too excited. Play football but don't do endless kicking as legs can be mistaken for a ball in the heat of the moment and receive a nip. Encourage gentle interaction and mind games and this will allow the child and the dog to build a mutually solid foundation of understanding.

Child or Children

I have referred to child, singular, and to children, plural, throughout the book and whilst writing I have pondered several times how to cover as many scenarios as possible. Only in the case of twins will there be two children equal in age and only if the children arrive after the dog will there be more than one small child and a dog. In previous chapters I have dealt with how to help the already established dog to understand and accept your children and how to educate young children to be respectful of your dog. Older teenagers are classed as adults when it comes to dog management, they are old enough to know right from wrong and should have enough common sense to know what is best for their dog. However, even they will benefit from books and family discussions of how best to educate the dog to everyone's advantage. Young teenagers are capable of having an adult relationship with a dog when it comes to training, general

LIVING, LOVING AND LEARNING TOGETHER

A different Hannah from our little friend who reads stories. This Hannah is learning all about dogs and how to behave with them. Rob knows that he must not use his teeth or be possessive with the ball so he pushes it towards Hannah inviting her to play. Should her right foot make contact with the ball he will immediately remove his foot.

quality time on their own with their dog. An only child will be used to this kind of relationship and will often relate to their dog as other children may relate to a best buddy. If there is more than one child in a family, arguments can arise as to who does what. Make sure that they all share responsibilities but do try to encourage individual as well as group interaction, don't allow your dog to be the centre of arguments, or in a tug of war for affections. The eldest child will probably be the best equipped to control the dog but the youngest one should be encouraged to help. To exclude the youngest from responsibility can result in the child being unaware of how to behave correctly with either your own or strange dogs at a later date.

Whose Dog Is It?

As the decision to have a dog in the first place must be a family decision then the dog must be the family dog. But that does not mean that one member of the family may not actually have a closer bond with the dog than other members. It is however wise to make sure that all members of the family know the situation before the dog arrives and with children it may have to be handled delicately. If it is mum or dad's dog a child will accept this far more readily than the dog belonging to a sister or a brother, yet if the dog belongs to all of the children arguments may ensue. When my children were young the dogs were family dogs belonging to me and I had the final say in their welfare. When my daughter was ten she was allowed a puppy but it was made clear to her that she must accept the responsibility for it. Lass lived to be twelve years old and was my

management and welfare but they also still have a wonderful imagination and a child's ability to live in a world of their own creation. In fact, is there any dog lover who hasn't sheltered under a tree in a rainstorm and felt a wonderful, albeit wet, feeling of oneness with their dog and nature? Don't deny your children this magic by discouraging them from having daughter's best friend and confidante. My son, two years younger, continued to help me with the 'family' dogs and was happy with this situation, he was not ready for the responsibility of a dog of his own until he was twelve. At the time of writing his dog Cas is thirteen years old, fit, healthy and living with my son and his partner. We were fortunate in having the space to accommodate more than one dog and my children were used to animals and so understood the responsibilities involved. My daughter was competitive and entered many competitions but my son had no interest in that whatsoever, however, he supported her and she never tried to involve him in her sport. They were never pushed into having a dog of their own, in fact I argued against it until I was sure that they knew what they were taking on. Neither were they ever pushed into competing – one wanted to and one didn't. But one thing I knew they would both do was look after the welfare of their dogs and make sure that they were never subjected to unwelcome advances from other children or adults.

Your children as individuals will have preferences and will not always agree but when it comes to a dog's welfare they must behave maturely, do what is best for the dog and learn to share responsibilities rather than argue about them.

One Dog or Two

I have touched on the subject of having a second dog earlier in the book and although it is a personal decision for each family I would beg anyone considering having a second dog to think very carefully. Yes, we had more than one dog and my children had their own dogs but dogs

This is very similar to the previous photograph with Hannah and Rob but my reason for using it is to point out Rob's body language. If you look at the previous picture where he is nearer to Hannah you will notice a sharper expression and a keener body position. In this picture although looking at him Hannah is further away and his attitude is more relaxed. This is a dog who knows that he must not jump up or use his teeth, but you can see how a dog that may not be so well behaved would become excited at the prospect of a game and when near to a child might jump up.

have always been a part of my life. We had the space for them and living with dogs was not a novelty for my children – they knew it could be hard work. Having a second dog does not make life easier because the first one has company; it makes life more difficult because you must be constantly making sure that the dogs are not forming their own pack. A dog will identify with another canine pal, they will play canine games and interact with each other roughly. If I were to imagine a scene that would make me nervous it would be several children playing, running round, shouting and screaming, and a dog running with them and yapping hysterically. But if I imagined that same scene with two dogs running and yapping hysterically I would be worried, especially if the dogs were large and strong and the children were young. These scenes do occur, accidents happen and we tend to think they happen to other people rather than to us. Two dogs can be wonderful but only if you know what you are doing – that is, if dog number one is 100 per cent well-behaved before you get dog number two; if you have the time, space and patience and, above all, if your children are not just good but excellent with dogs.

Something to Think About

I get asked many questions regarding dog training and behaviour and below are some of the most frequent ones regarding dogs and children with my answers.

Is there a breed to be recommended for children?

I would never recommend any particular breed although there are some that are more unsuitable than others. Careful thought to what you want and what you can provide must be coupled with careful selection of temperament and character.

Should I allow my dog to own its bed?

Yes, it needs a safe haven. If you train it correctly and you are the pack leader it will expect you to provide it with a place of its own to sleep. Several cases spring to mind of dogs that have not been allowed to own their bed and children who have been bitten when they have gone near. This has occurred simply because the dog has been fed up with being invaded and has felt it had no choice but to decide itself what it could and could not own. You must be the provider and a well-trained dog will respect your rules and your children.

Can my dog have a bone?

Only in its own area and children must leave it in peace.

My dog's routine will change during the school holidays, does this matter?

Routines are fine as long as we don't become a slave to them, the change during the holiday will not be so much of a problem as when the children go back to school. Try to make sure your dog retains some of its 'normal' routine each day and lengthen it as the holiday nears its end.

Is there anything that may seem harmless to me but that could cause problems?

Toy guns, cap guns, balloons and anything else that bangs can bring great pleasure to children but can terrify a dog. Also water holds a fascination for many children, particularly if your dog likes swimming and splashing, but a ball or stick thrown too far can put a dog in jeopardy and any child that tries to rescue it. A dog splashing in water can soon knock a child off balance and even shallow water can then become dangerous.

My children love hugging my dog, does this matter?

Provided your dog is clean and doesn't object, there is no problem. But you must make it perfectly clear to your children that what is acceptable to your dog may not be to another dog. They may hug you goodnight but they would not hug a total stranger, your dog is within your family unit and what happens in this unit is not necessarily what happens with people (or dogs) outside that unit. I would strongly recommend that you discourage your dog from licking your children's hands and faces.

Does it make any difference whether I have a male or a female dog?

It is the dog that matters, not its gender. Bitches can often be more motherly but they can also be more possessive. Dogs may not be as possessive but if they are, they can be more dominant. Each one will balance against the other, some people may prefer one sex to the other but really it is the dog itself that is important, not colour, gender or shape.

If my dog is lower in the pack than my children will it guard them?

Think of this another way. If you are at home and someone knocks on the door your dog will bark to let you know someone is there. When you invite that person into your home your dog will accept this. If you are out and an intruder enters your home your dog will not necessarily accept this and will protect your home.

All dogs are different, some will bark and bite a burglar and some may try and lick them to death! If a dog is protective, it will usually protect children in danger; this is not nasty or possessive but a loyal dog looking after the interests of the pack and those within it. If you are not there to protect them and it feels that the children, although higher in status, are not able to defend themselves it will close ranks and defend them. My daughter went for a walk one evening taking Lass with her and a motorcyclist stopped to ask directions, Lass growled and moved in between my daughter and the cyclist – needless to say he departed rather rapidly. But never assume that your dog will protect as a matter of course. My children rarely went anywhere without their dogs but this didn't mean they could go further afield; it just meant I worried about them 99 per cent instead of 100 per cent.

Other Dogs and Other Children

If you have brought your children up to understand dogs and to respect them as individual beings you should never have a problem with other people's dogs. Your children will know that they should not approach a strange dog without permission and they will know the correct approach if given permission. At no time should either adult or child approach an unknown dog that is tied up. This dog is not only an unknown quantity it may feel either vulnerable or threatened if approached by strangers. You may know that you mean it no harm but there is no guarantee that you can convey that message to the dog. Neither do you know the temperament of the dog and what kind of a reception you or your children may get if you continue to enter its space.

Strangers approaching your dog may not be so easy to deal with especially if the strangers are children. At the end of the day you owe your loyalty to your dog and your family. You cannot be held responsible for the lack of canine education in other children but you will be held responsible for any adverse consequences should they approach your dog and either upset it or be on the receiving end of a nip. If you have any doubts at all as to the gentleness and knowledge of the approaching child or of your dog's attitude to him, stop him from advancing any further. You have the choice of either allowing him to come to your dog under your guidance or of telling him not to come any nearer. This is your dog and is part of your family, you would not let total strangers approach your children so think carefully before you allow your dog to make a contact he may not want to be introduced to.

Kids and dogs do go together but only if all are prepared to work at it. These dogs, Alice, Shani, Gemma, Floss and Nell, are all the same breed but they are not to be considered any better or any worse than a different breed. They are not good, bad or indifferent with children. They are dogs and are well trained and Becky is just as well-behaved as the dogs she is sitting with.

LIVING, LOVING AND LEARNING TOGETHER

A Special Bond

The most wonderful bond can be formed between a dog and a child but it is not something you can expect as part of the package of owning a dog and having children. Children need to confide, they share secrets, they spend time in an imaginary world and they may often talk about things to each other about which they know nothing at all but enjoy games of pretence. Teenagers need to have someone to share their troubles with, they need someone who will not relate all their inner feelings to the first adult they see and they need someone with whom they can still be a child without fear of losing their 'street cred'. A child will have groups of friends to share secrets with but over a period of time there will be fallings-out and confidences betrayed until eventually a bond is formed with one close friend. But when the friend has gone home for the night and the doors are closed who is there to turn to who will listen to either child or teenage troubles, not answer back, suggest a solution or tell them to 'act their age'? Big or small, pedigree or crossbreed if a dog has formed a bond with a human being, young or old, they will always be there for them and will always listen to them. Whether a child has a large group of friends or just one friend, brothers and sisters or is an only one, lives in a built-up area or out in the 'sticks', if they have a special canine friend they will never be alone.

Playing games with dogs may be good fun but they don't last; at the end of a game of ball what happens? Does the dog get pushed to the back of the mind of the child playing with it because it is no longer part of the entertainment? Or is the game a shared pastime that could be dispensed with quite happily, if the dog were unwell or age prevented its participation, for quieter and more sedate shared moments? The former indicates a youngster who is taking and not giving, the latter indicates friendship and loyalty.

Growing up with a dog can be a wonderful learning curve for life, it

Don't expect miracles, you have to work hard and then allow a friendship to blossom. Hannah is on the cover of this book with Skye. She has been taught to approach a dog from the side not to put her face to the dog's and to be gentle. But here she is with Rob, happy in his company and young though she is, she is learning how to care.

teaches trust, responsibility, loyalty and awareness of others' feelings. It is not just about games, toys, balls and having a good time. When you are young, there are times when all the world seems to be against you, times when you really cannot imagine what your parents are going to say about your latest catastrophe and times when you just want to run away from it all. Through it all there will be a pair of soulful eyes, a wet nose and a welcome tail wag from the little four-legged 'see all, hear all, and say nothing' best friend. Believe me I have cried into a dog's coat far more times than I have cried onto a human shoulder. As a child I told my dog everything, as a teenager my dog 'understood' perfectly well that a boyfriend could be wonderful one day and the worst man on earth the next. As an adult I am extremely grateful that my dogs cannot read, write or talk, as they may be tempted to hold me to ransom over my inner secrets!

A special bond with a dog is not guaranteed, it is dependent on the dog having the right temperament and the human being creating an empathy with it, like good parenting it is not easy but it is well worth the effort. If a child is not willing to make the effort then he is not ready for a dog, if a parent is not prepared to make the effort and to ensure that their child does likewise then the family is not ready for a dog. If the reason for wanting a dog is for the 'I' factor, I want to play, run, walk, compete, with my dog, the dog will never be able to give completely because humans will never stop taking. If the reason for wanting a dog is for love, companionship, the willingness to give and acceptance of some self sacrifice, the dog will give and keep on giving. That's what dogs do best.

Magic Moments

The first time a dog sits for its young handler is almost as good as baby's first words. To see a dog stand back at a doorway or a staircase making sure it does not push or squash its young master or mistress is when you know your dog respects and values your family. When your dog gently places a ball in front of your child when two moments before it was racing round like a supercharged running machine you will know your child is in safe paws. When you go upstairs at night and your dog is asleep outside your son or daughter's bedroom door, when he is waiting quietly by the door when they are due home from school, when he is as quiet as a mouse when one of them is unwell, when all of these come together in one dog and one relationship you know you have done it right.

When a poorly child feels a soft nose nuzzle his hand, the pain will ease a little. When a teenager looks into his dog's soulful brown eyes believing that all the world is against him, he knows that he will never be alone. When children go fishing for whatever they think they might find in a dirty puddle and their dog diligently helps them, they know that they have a buddy. When their best friend lets them down they know they have a true best friend waiting to hear all about it and see them through the bad times. This is true dog companionship, anything else is settling for less than 100 per cent, the companionship of a dog and the knowledge that it will never let you down is worth its weight in gold. This is what children need teaching. Not how to throw a ball, play games and dig in a sand pit – these are extras and will become a part of life after the friendship has blossomed.

LIVING, LOVING AND LEARNING TOGETHER

Don't expect miracles, but work hard and with determination, and stick to what you know needs to be done throughout any tantrums or 'Oh buts' and 'I'll do it tomorrows' from your offspring. Give as much consideration to your dog as to your children. After all, it didn't ask to join your family – you chose it. Teach your children to have patience and compassion with your dog, it will hold them in good stead in later life. Above all, teach them to honour and love your dog for once they begin to see him as a thinking, feeling being they are on their way to understanding other animals and nature.

If you teach your dog and your children how to enjoy life together in harmony you may find that you are the loser. For what you gain in the satisfaction of seeing them together and understanding one another, you will lose when you are excluded from their 'secrets'. They will always be 'up to something' and you will probably be the last to know what it is. You may have to accept they will be inseparable so prepare for camping or caravan holidays and when they consider you too old to understand don't be offended, just be glad your dog won't be leading your child astray.

When your youngster decides to go to bed early, make sure you check under the covers when he is asleep, you may just find a smuggled dog there. Be prepared to have to cater for two when they poddle down the garden together for a picnic, and make it quite clear to your child that digging up and eating grubs like the dog is unacceptable – they do share everything you know. Oh and don't forget *you* will never understand your child as well as your dog does, you may have given birth to him, nursed him, had sleepless nights and spent an absolute fortune on him but that dog will put you in the shade!

This picture says it all. For Skye and Hannah this is a moment in time when the whole world stands still and nothing else matters. It only lasts for a second but it is worth a fortune. A child sharing a delight with a friend, a dog who can trust the child not to do anything to upset her. Sam, Hannah's mother, Malcolm and Maureen who were taking the photographs and myself, all were watching and not one of us was included in this moment. Who knows what secret they shared – it was their magic moment.

But it's worth it all, even though you may begin to feel a little bit jealous of the way they leave you out of their conversations and of the way they seem so right together. In fact you may decide it's time you introduced another dog into the family, one for *you* to confide in. But I will tell you right now that no matter how magical a relationship you may have with it you will never again touch what you had when you were young and what your child is enjoying.

Each stage of our lives brings with it something special and it is up to us to discover it. You must create a different empathy with your dog, for the one your child will share with his dog is part of the secret of youth. It is a wonderful world of imagination, where feelings are not hidden, where love is given unconditionally and emotions are not hidden. It is all the colours of the rainbow, just as magical and just as good to see.

So you see all the forethought, the hard work and the patience will be worth it. You will watch your children grow up in harmony with nature and they will reap the benefit of a wonderful four-legged companion to share their magical moments with.

INDEX

aggression 51, 66, 75, 79

baby 12–13, 17–18, 20–21, 32–35, 38–39, 44, 46–47, 50–57, 90
balls 60, 68, 89
beds 40, 42–50, 541 56, 62, 65–67, 77, 80, 82, 86, 91
biting 41
bones 17–18, 28, 44, 53, 57, 86
breed 13, 15, 22–24, 37, 39, 41, 47, 49, 52–55, 66, 68–71, 86, 89

car 13, 15, 20, 30, 61, 67, 80
chasing 28, 60–62, 68

excited 10, 22, 44, 68, 72–73, 75, 79, 83

games 10, 28, 47–48, 50, 58, 60, 62, 67, 77, 81, 83, 86, 89–90
guarding 87

holidays 12, 86, 91
hugging 87
hysteria 39, 61, 68

jealousy 11, 28, 32, 34–35, 37, 39, 48, 53, 55–56, 65, 70

kennels 25, 69

large dogs 23, 37, 60, 69, 86
licking 63, 87

littermates 67, 77

nipping 59–60, 63, 67–68

older dogs 24, 28

playing 10, 19, 32, 35, 37, 39, 40, 48, 50, 55, 60, 66–68, 73, 82, 86, 89
praise 55
pulling 24, 57, 60, 79
puppies 23, 37, 40, 67

recall 27, 66
rescue 15, 24–26, 41, 69, 87
roundup 68
routine 12–13, 20, 34, 38, 53, 86

small dogs 23, 37, 47, 60, 68
squeaky toys 53, 58
strangers 40, 65, 79, 88

teenagers 47, 50, 83, 89
titbits 29, 62–63, 73
toddler 11, 13, 17, 30, 44, 46–47, 52, 54–58, 63
toys 13, 18–19, 28, 47–48, 53, 55–58, 60, 90
training 9, 11–13, 15, 21–22, 24–28, 39, 44–45, 50, 55, 62, 66–69, 77–78, 80, 84, 86
tug 56, 60, 75, 79, 84